CIVIC LITERACY
Through
CURRICULUM DRAMA
Grades 6–12

Catherine A. Franklin

CORWIN PRESS
A SAGE Company

For information:

Corwin Press
A SAGE Company
2455 Teller Road
Thousand Oaks, California 91320
www.corwinpress.com

SAGE Ltd.
1 Oliver's Yard
55 City Road
London EC1Y 1SP
United Kingdom

SAGE India Pvt. Ltd.
B 1/I 1 Mohan Cooperative
  Industrial Area
Mathura Road, New Delhi 110 044
India

SAGE Asia-Pacific Pte. Ltd.
33 Pekin Street #02-01
Far East Square
Singapore 048763

Printed in the United States of America.

Library of Congress Cataloging-in-Publication Data

Franklin, Catherine A.
Civil literacy through curriculum drama, grades 6–12/Catherine A. Franklin.
    p. cm.
Includes bibliographical references and index.
ISBN 978-1-4129-3928-7 (cloth)
ISBN 978-1-4129-3929-4 (pbk.)
    1. Social sciences—Study and teaching (Middle school)—United States—Curricula.
2. Social sciences—Study and teaching (Secondary)—United States—Curricula.
3. Drama in education—United States. 4. Constructivism (Education)—United States. 5. Imagination in children. I. Title.

H62.5.U5F715 2009
300.71′2—dc22   2008022892

This book is printed on acid-free paper.

08   09   10   11   12   10   9   8   7   6   5   4   3   2   1

Acquisitions Editor:	Cathy Hernandez
Editorial Assistant:	Ena Rosen
Production Editor:	Libby Larson
Copy Editor:	Cate Huisman
Typesetter:	C&M Digitals (P) Ltd.
Proofreader:	Susan Schon
Indexer:	Kathy Paparchontis
Cover Designer:	Monique Hahn
Graphic Designer:	Anthony Paular

Contents

List of Tables and Figures

Tables

Figures

Preface

At a time when our nation's public schools are narrowly defined by reading and math scores, scripted curriculum, and high-stakes tests, and students are becoming more and more disconnected to the school environment, there is an urgent need to show how curriculum can be engaging, rigorous, and relevant to the lives of the children and the families it serves.

Curriculum drama provides an innovative way for teachers and students to become invested in the world within a curricular area, to develop complex understandings within a content area, and to engage in purposeful collaboration with each other. With its participatory structure, curriculum drama helps to develop students' sense of agency, creating an environment where they can appraise the world around them, and in their constructed classroom positions, they can take deliberative action. Now more than ever, we need our students to develop experience as informed leaders and as critically minded, socially conscious citizens.

Purpose

Civic Literacy Through Curriculum Drama describes an innovative approach for engaging students in the lived world of social studies. Field tested in various classrooms—public and private, at various academic levels—from middle schools to a university setting, "curriculum drama" (Franklin, 2003) creates a pedagogical bridge that connects student interests with curricular content.

Without scripted roles or predetermined outcomes, the teacher *and* the students construct the curriculum drama. Through this process, students develop a new frame of reference within the classroom. They interact with each other, not in their conventional classroom roles as students, but rather from constructed positions within a defined community of practice. For example, they study the legislative process by working *as senators* in their classroom senate (Chapters 3–8); they closely analyze the "crimes" of a literary character in a novel (or historical figure) by transforming the class to a courtroom and working *as members of the criminal judicial system* (Chapter 8).

Who Should Read This Book?

Middle and secondary school educators who teach social studies or those who want to situate social studies as a core topic within the extended literacy program will find this book helpful, relevant, and thought provoking. Teachers of adolescents know that students yearn to be engaged with the world, and they need the opportunity to talk back to society. Curriculum drama provides them with an appropriate structure within which to develop leadership skills, take initiative, and engage in peer collaboration. In addition, curriculum coordinators, parent groups, and directors of afterschool programs will be well served by the many classroom ideas presented in this book.

Furthermore, this text has relevance at the college and university levels. Whether the topic is history, political science, literature, or speech, faculty can use curriculum drama as a way to teach. In this way, students will be motivated to develop complex understandings in a content area through their inside positions within this constructed experience. In teacher preparation programs, particularly those in social studies education, English education, curriculum design, or educational drama, this book provides a window into constructivist practice.

Step-by-Step Approach

Many teachers recognize the power of experiential learning, but they do not know how to successfully prepare their classrooms for this transformation. This text provides a hands-on guide. One of the curriculum dramas explored in this text is the classroom senate. Chapters 3–8 suggest steps for transforming the classroom to a legislative setting. For easy access, I list the key topics, the format of the experience (e.g., full class session, small groups) and the approximate number of class sessions. As this is a constructed experience, not a scripted one, this "plan of action" is merely a guide; included in this section are shortcuts and extensions to custom-design the experience for any time frame. A resource section at the end of this book includes activity sheets, project guidelines, and samples of student work.

Making Classroom Dilemmas Transparent

This text, however, goes far beyond being a "how to" guide. I wrote it from the vantage point of a classroom teacher who has taught a diverse range of students in both public and private school settings around the world and who is now a teacher educator at an urban public university working with the next generation of new educators.

I have spiced this book with dilemmas that students and I encountered when we used this approach in our classroom. For example, in Chapter 4, I describe an encounter with collective student resistance. In Chapter 5, I recount an episode when students as senators decided to take a spontaneous recess. Chapters 6–8 describe other classroom glitches. Making these challenges transparent underscores the inherent nature of curriculum drama. It can be unpredictable, and at times it can feel like a ride on the wild side!

These dilemmas, however, stretched my own practice (and patience). I grew from these experiences, and I believe my teaching became better. Along with describing these unexpected moments in the classroom, this text also explores how as a class the students and I worked together to address these credibility issues and how we devised strategies to bring collective belief back into the classroom situation.

Chapter Summaries

Chapter 1, "Curriculum Drama: An Engaging Approach to Social Studies," describes the constructive nature of this classroom approach, its relevance to standards in social studies and language arts, and its emergence within the field of educational drama. Chapter 2, "Constructing Curriculum Drama: Exploring Its Structure," describes how teachers can construct their own curriculum dramas by using three processes: adapting content from a blueprint (e.g., using a primary document), setting the stage (e.g., stimulating visual curiosity), and devising multiple entry points (i.e., creating situations).

Chapters 3–8 examine an extended curriculum drama focused on the legislative branch of government. Each chapter builds upon the one before it. Chapter 3, "Becoming a Senator: Setting the Stage," explores the preliminary tasks involved in helping students construct their frame of reference as senators. Chapter 4, "Political Parties: Building Belief," and Chapter 5, "Holding an Election: Engaging in Multiple Entry Points," describe how to construct a political world within the legislative experience. Chapter 6, "Current Events: Doing Legislative Work," builds upon current events as a way for students to construct legislation based on issues that are meaningful to them. Chapter 7, "Constructing a Hearing: Appraising Witness Testimony," shows the classroom transformation to a legislative hearing. Chapter 8, "Constructing a Debate: Taking Legislative Action," examines how students as senators take a public stance on prioritized legislation.

Chapter 9, "Constructing Curriculum Drama in Other Contexts," describes ways to use this approach in current events, history, and law. The first example outlines ways to transform the classroom to a world summit on peace; students interact *as leaders of peace* to devise plans for civic action and community building. The second examines the women's suffrage movement in the nineteenth century; students *as concerned citizens* engage in a town hall meeting to debate whether women should have the right to vote. The final example details the construction of a criminal trial as a way to build deep understanding about our judicial system; students *as members of a jury* determine the fate of a literary character (or historical figure).

Ideas for Reading This Text

There are many ways to read this book. Some may prefer to go cover to cover and read the chapters in sequential order. For these readers, the first two chapters describe curriculum drama and its conceptual framework, how it reflects attention to national standards in social studies and English language arts, and how internal structures work to develop the experience. The middle chapters bring to life an extended curriculum drama in a particular field of civics (i.e., legislative practice). The final chapter explores the use of curriculum drama in such content areas as current events, history, and the criminal justice system.

For those who are social studies teachers seeking to engage students in a study of the legislative branch of government, Chapters 3–8 will be particularly useful. These chapters provide a detailed approach for constructing a classroom senate. Chapters 4 and 5 take a detour from lawmaking to add a political layer to the context. These two chapters include *suggested* experiences; if you are under scheduling constraints, you may decide to read these chapters for background purposes only and concentrate on Chapters 3, 6, 7, and 8.

Others may be interested in exploring curriculum drama as a concept and how it can be designed in different areas of social studies or language arts; in this instance, Chapters 1, 2, 3, and 9 will be particularly relevant.

Civic Literacy Through Curriculum Drama provides an innovative way to make social studies accessible, relevant, and fun. This book challenges teachers and administrators alike to explore the power of imagination and the use of active inquiry within the classroom setting. By examining the processes that help to shape curriculum drama (Chapters 1 and 2), by learning how to build an ongoing situation within the classroom (Chapters 3–8), and by exploring other contexts for curriculum drama (Chapter 9), teachers will be well positioned to begin the process of constructing engaging curricular experiences within their own classrooms.

Acknowledgments

The energy of supportive colleagues and inquisitive students has made all the difference in my teaching practice. Various schools have provided me with opportunities to create new curriculum, build upon existing curriculum, and construct curriculum with students. I am grateful to the colleagues and students at Bank Street School for Children and the intermediate school City College Academy of the Arts (CCAA). At Bank Street, I thank former Dean Rudy Jordan for helping to pave the way for this endeavor. I also owe a special debt of gratitude to Sam Brian, my colleague for a number of years, for generously sharing curriculum resources, his expertise in social studies and his insightful perspectives on classroom practice. Most recently at CCAA, it has been an honor to consult with faculty on curriculum drama in a public school setting. I thank Professor Joyce Coppin, Dr. Burnedette Drysdale, and Judith Ghinger for their leadership and vision. At the same time, I thank Llewellyn Somers and Aminta Nuñez for welcoming me into their classroom and helping to transform it to a senate experience. Internationally, I am grateful that I was able to begin my teaching practice at the Colegio Nueva Granada in Bogotá, Colombia, and that several years later I had the opportunity to consult with faculty on social studies curriculum at the Rato Bangala School in Kathmandu, Nepal.

At The City College of the City University of New York, I thank Dean Alfred S. Posamentier and Associate Dean Doris Cintrón for being constant champions of my work. Professor Gretchen Johnson, chair of the Department of Childhood Education, reviewed an earlier draft of this manuscript and provided me with timely suggestions and ideas. Several years ago I had the great fortune to team teach with Professor Harriet Alonso, peace historian in the Department of History, who remains a trusted advisor. I also want to acknowledge that this work was supported in part by a grant from The City University of New York PSC-CUNY Research Award Program.

At Teachers College, Columbia University, I wish to express my gratitude to Celia Genishi, Marjorie Siegel, and Karen Zumwalt. I appreciate the support, guidance, and trust they extended as I began this long journey.

I thank Corwin Press for helping to shepherd this book through the stages of production. Special thanks to editor Cathy Hernandez for her support, experience, and insight, and to Cate Huisman for her diligence and sensitivity as copyeditor. I am grateful to Corwin's reviewers; I referred back to their comments countless times as I explored new directions during the revision process.

I first explored a number of the concepts in this book in works published over the past few years. I thank Jonathan Silin and the editorial board of the Occasional Paper Series for helping me to develop a monograph for their publication and to Catherine Fosnot for asking me to write a chapter for her book *Constructivism: Theory, Perspectives, and Practice* (2005).

I also thank the following people for their help along the way: Roberta Berman, Michael Cook, Harriet Cuffaro, Kathryn Daniels, Jay Heubert, Irene Roberts, Toby Weinberger, and Michael Wilkinson.

Finally, I thank my family for their steady confidence, support, and love.

CAF

Publisher's Acknowledgments

Corwin Press gratefully acknowledges the contributions of the following reviewers:

Carrie Ames
Social Studies Teacher
Gallup High School
Gallup, NM

Thomas Best
Instructor, Secondary Social
   Studies
Monmouth College
Social Studies Teacher
Central Jr. High, Monmouth, IL

D. Antonio Cantu
Professor and Dean
   of Education
Indiana University Kokomo
Kokomo, IN

Leslie Carmel-Porras
NBCT, Social Studies
   Teacher
Silverado High School
Las Vegas, NV

Karen Chenoweth
Social Studies Department
    Chair and Teacher
Pine Ridge High School
Deltona, FL

Michael Crull
Social Studies Teacher
West Jay Middle School
Muncie, IN

Toni Dekiere-Phillips
Social Studies Teacher
Rockdale County High
Conyers, GA

Susan Gogue
Social Studies Department
    Chair and Teacher
Jack Young Middle School
Baraboo, WI

Gayla LeMay
Social Studies and U.S. History
    Teacher
Louise Radloff Middle
    School
Duluth, GA

Denise Mullen
Social Studies Department
    Chair and Teacher
James Monroe Middle School
Albuquerque, NM

Lisa Satterfield
Social Studies Teacher
Jason Lee Middle School
Vancouver, WA

George Thomson
U.S. Government Teacher
Nogales High School
Nogales, AZ

Julie Wakefield
Geography Teacher
McQueen High School
Reno, NV

Marian White-Hood
Director of Academics,
    Accountability, and
    Principal Support
Maya Angelou Public Charter
    Schools and the See Forever
    Foundation
Washington, DC

About the Author

 **Catherine A. Franklin** is an assistant professor in the School of Education at The City College of the City University of New York. She teaches social studies education to both undergraduates and graduates. She began her career by teaching in schools around the world (e.g., Colombia, Japan). In New York City, she was a middle school classroom teacher for over 10 years. Along with teaching social studies, literature, and writing to eighth grade students, she worked as a cooperating teacher for student teachers who were placed in her classroom. She earned her EdD at Teachers College, Columbia University, in the Department of Curriculum and Teaching and her MA in International Education from Lesley University. She consults on social studies education and curriculum design.

To my intrepid students,
from past years,
present times,
and future encounters.
CF

1

Curriculum Drama

An Engaging Approach to Social Studies

The senate chamber bustled to life as preoccupied members of Congress arrived for a pivotal legislative session. Walking toward their seats, some were hailed by waiting colleagues and huddled in groups for private conversations. Others walked directly to their seats to review their prepared statements and to read over the latest updates on the bill they were to debate on the senate floor.

The week before, the Environmental Affairs Committee had shepherded the Clean Air Act through a somewhat contentious hearing process, and committee members were anxious to bring the legislation to a vote.

With the decisive tap of the gavel against the table, the leader called the session to order. The buzz of conversations diminished, and there was momentary silence. Then the debate began.

Sen. Santos: I plan to ratify the Clean Air Act. I feel that the nation's air being clean far outweighs the bill's drawbacks. I yield the floor.

Sen. Blitz: I disagree with my colleague, Sen. Santos. I plan on voting against this legislation. This bill requires factories to use a filter that currently costs $100 million. To keep businesses running and to be in compliance with this legislation, factory owners will have to fire people so as to keep their profit margins up. Ruining people's lives is not the answer for clean air.

Sen. Provia: We should be more concerned about the future than with saving jobs. I plan to vote for this bill.

These senators were not current members of Congress but were classmates participating in a middle school social studies class. Jorge Santos, Mike Blitz, and Emma Provia (all names in this text are pseudonyms) engaged in an intense debate about the feasibility of this environmental legislation. Students explored this issue not from the outside looking in, as mere readers of a civics text on the legislative branch of government, but rather as engaged participants from the inside, as senators concerned with the bottom line of a proposed law. To read details of this legislation, refer to the resource section at the back of this book; Resource I contains details of this student-made bill.

Civic Literacy Through Curriculum Drama, Grades 6–12 draws from real classrooms with real students. It describes an innovative approach called "curriculum drama" (Franklin, 2003) that engages students in the core practice and mindful activity of related fields within the social studies. Without predetermined outcomes or scripted roles, curriculum drama emerges from the power of student and teacher constructions to a place where class members interact as insiders within a field of practice.

This text provides classroom tested ideas for constructing curriculum drama. Flexible in design, curriculum drama can be constructed for any area of social studies. Chapter 2 describes the inner workings of this approach, so readers can build a viable experience within their own classrooms.

Readers may enjoy examining a detailed account of how to construct an extended curriculum drama on the legislative branch of government. Along with a weekly outline highlighting key tasks and situated events, I have also included ideas on how to extend (or abridge) this experience. In this section I use the created voices of one particular class of students. Essentially, this is a composite sketch drawn from my many years of classroom experience, both in the United States and overseas, where I have successfully used this approach to engage a range of students in understanding units of study within the social studies (see Chapters 3–8).

Readers may also be interested in understanding how curriculum drama can be designed in other social studies areas. Along with the classroom senate, I have included ideas for designing curriculum dramas in current events, history, and law (see Chapter 9). Use of this classroom approach is limited only by your imagination and the imaginations of your students.

This book also includes descriptions of those situations when curriculum drama stuttered, stalled, or fell into a state of disarray within the classroom. How do the students and I, their teacher, work together to bring credibility and rigor back into the experience? To understand these dilemmas and how we worked through them, readers may want to explore "classroom dilemmas" (see Chapters 4–8).

Can Curriculum Drama Work in Your Classroom?

Curriculum drama is an approach to teaching and learning that can work successfully in a range of educational settings. I have constructed curriculum dramas for classes at the middle school level to the college level, in public and private school settings, in classrooms where there is great student homogeneity and in classrooms where there is a wide range of student diversity. I have seen young adults actively engage in curriculum drama who have been classified as emergent English language learners and/or have individualized education programs. I have used this approach for remedial learners and for precocious students.

Whether your school is located in an economically poor urban neighborhood, a working middle class community, or an exclusive suburb, this approach to teaching and learning will be an unforgettable and educative experience for your students. Curriculum drama works within flexible time frames and is highly adaptable to various settings.

Understanding Curriculum Drama

Curriculum drama forms a bridge that links the tasks of teaching, learning, and inquiry to the authentic interests, concerns, and energies of the students. This approach pulls the class together into new ways of being, knowing, and interacting within "the lived situations of life" (Dewey, 1934, p. 263). In this way, students generate complex understandings *as insiders* to the defined unit of study.

Breaking Out of the Conventional

Curriculum drama disrupts the taken-for-granted ways of classroom interactions. Individuals break out of conventional classroom roles and work with each other and the curriculum in new ways. Activities take on a deeper meaning, and students become motivated to learn more about a topic not because of an impending test, but because they have become deeply engaged in its relevance.

For instance, in the case of the legislative drama, students as senators become motivated to conduct research and devise their own legislation based on national, regional, and/or personal concerns about contemporary society. Working in committee, they discuss and revise this legislation. In this way, students become provoked to use the power of imagination to "reach beyond where they are" (Greene, 2005, p. 116) as young members of society.

At the same time, curriculum drama helps to situate individuals in a learning context that matters. Within the legislative drama, students as senators engage in lawmaking activities, and they live through the consequences of their collective, legislative decisions. This participatory experience connects students with one another, and, at the same time, it challenges the individual to develop informed positions and to envision possible solutions about the issues that confront society.

A Coconstructed Process

Curriculum drama is a coconstructed process. Rather than being directed, powered, or shaped by the adult in charge, students are partners in the construction process. Freed from following any preexisting story line, students have a broad landscape, albeit within a defined context, to explore their roles as members of an emerging community within the classroom setting.

Through the course of this experience, students become involved in lived inquiries that reflect "real topics contemplated in everyday life" (Kuhn, 1986, p. 501). For instance, reflecting upon the senate debate and the cost factors involved with the Clean Air Act, one student wrote,

> We are saying how we feel pretty much. I mean we know about the situation. We know about our economy and how we are in debt. I mean some people might have had their parents lose jobs and how hard it is to get another one. We realize how hard it is for them. We don't want people to lose their jobs. We are really thinking about this stuff. We are doing this from our own experience. (Katie)

Because it is coconstructed by teacher and student engagement, negotiation, and activity, curriculum drama puts into practice constructivist pedagogy. Brooks and Brooks (1993) list five guiding principles for a constructivist approach (p. 33), and these principles are weaved throughout the lifespan of an ongoing curriculum drama:

- Posing problems of emerging relevance to students
- Structuring learning around primary concepts
- Seeking and valuing students' points of view
- Adapting curriculum to address students' suppositions
- Assessing student learning in the context of teaching

Learning New Ways of Being

While there is certainly an imaginary element to curriculum drama, in that the class is envisioning itself not as students but as inside participants of a defined community, this approach is grounded in real world issues and pragmatic applications. This provides an appropriate way for young adolescents to develop experience in taking a public stance and talking back to the world. Moreover, they engage in efforts not only to appraise the world around them and identify complex problems facing contemporary society but to work together to take responsible action to address these issues. In the case of the classroom senate, they gain both access to and insight into how democratic structures function within our system of government.

Shift in Classroom Roles

In curriculum drama the class members move away from their predictable positions as students and teacher to interacting in an entirely new context. For instance, in a curriculum drama based on the legislative branch of government, students work as senators to construct legislation. In this setting, the teacher may strategically decide to work as senate clerk, senior advisor, or political consultant. In a curriculum drama designed around a historical event, the class might decide to transform the room to a courtroom and work in legal teams to bring charges against a controversial leader. In this setting, the teacher might decide to interact as judge, bailiff, or legal counsel. Or for yet another example, in current events the class could receive an invitation to attend a "World Summit on Peace." Each student could then conduct research on a well-known advocate for peace and work to construct a way to represent that individual for this upcoming event. Within this context, the teacher might work as lead conference planner, keynote speaker, or news reporter.

Shift in Classroom Texts

Along with a shift in classroom roles, the position of the textbook moves as well. Rather than being at the center of teacher-student activity, it is now used as one of several frames of reference. For instance, in the classroom senate, students use their civics textbook to examine the U.S. Constitution, Article 1 (legislative branch) for ideas on how to construct their senate. In their criminal trial of a historical figure, students use their history books to access primary documents (e.g., speeches, declarations) that can serve as evidence in their legal case and use the Bill of Rights (e.g., rights of the accused) to structure their trial. With preparations for the World Summit in their current events drama, the class could report on current news articles or images that relate in some way to peace or the need for peace.

Shift in Teacher and Student Relationships

In curriculum drama, students and their teacher work in concert and negotiate with one another. While there are shifts in classroom roles and status, this does not imply that the teacher has given up adult authority. But rather, the teacher collaboratively works with the class to build collective belief in this new classroom environment.

At times, curriculum drama makes strategic leaps into the world of imagination. Within this realm, both the students and their teacher step into and take seriously their constructed positions, responsibilities, and status. At other times, curriculum drama takes a leap back into the classroom setting. Taking off their constructed roles, the class reflects upon this classroom drama and draws comparisons to its counterpart in society (or history).

Curriculum drama is placed alongside the topic under study. Students move away from *studying about* a topic as detached observers to *learning within* the topic as informed insiders. The class works on tasks within a constructed community of practice that is aligned in some way to key concepts and facts within the intended focus.

Like an Accordion in Design

Curriculum drama can fit into varying time frames and schedules. For instance, as a social studies teacher I have teamed with the English language arts teacher to create a purposeful block of time with my students. I have designed curriculum drama at other schools, where social studies is scheduled throughout the week in both 45 minute and 90 minute periods. Curriculum drama could even be organized as an ongoing Friday afternoon event. Obviously, the more time that can be devoted to this approach, the more likely students will take it seriously and will take ownership of it. In this way, they will develop complex understandings from the experience. Curriculum drama thrives in those settings where there is genuine attention placed on providing an educational environment, not a scripted one, and where students have the time to truly engage in the business of deep learning.

Using Curriculum Drama to Meet Standards

Curriculum drama, with its emphasis on peer interactions, participatory learning, and active use of imagination and inquiry, is well suited to adolescent and adult learners. This approach to teaching and learning has the potential to disrupt the prevailing climate of social alienation and academic disengagement that has too often characterized the educational experience for our nation's students (Juvonen, Le, Kaganoff, Augustine, & Constant, 2004).

At the same time, this approach brings to the fore the relevancy of social studies content and the need to critically inquire about the world. Sadly, one of the unintended consequences of recent educational policy at the federal level is the narrowing of curricular focus and teaching within the school day (Neill, 2003) so as to prepare students for high-stakes tests in reading and math. The field of social studies in particular has been seriously marginalized with this current testing frenzy (VanFossen, 2005; von Zastrow & Janc, 2004).

Classrooms, particularly at the middle and secondary school levels, have become disconnected environments where the emphasis is placed not on students but rather on performance outcomes numerically measured by paper-and-pencil tests during a timed session. In compliance with current educational policy, many schools relegate our students to peering *at* the world through the fuzzy lens of scripted curriculum or from assigned chapter readings from a textbook. With mounting pressures to go along with the ever present and ever changing climate of top-down mandates, our nation's schools run the risk of placing social studies on the back burner or worse still in a locked and forgotten storage room!

The field of social studies works to teach students to be critically minded and to take active notice of the world so as to participate as informed citizens. Freire (1973) reminds us that "to be human is to engage in relationships *with* others and *with* the world" (p. 3) (italics mine). Social studies is a unique field of study in that it pays close attention to the human experience. This connects to its purpose as a discipline, as noted by the National Council for the Social Studies:

> The primary purpose of social studies is to help young people develop the ability to make informed and reasoned decisions for the public good as citizens of a culturally diverse, democratic society in an interdependent world. (1994, p. 3)

Students and their teachers need time to examine the world and to engage with the world in both a rigorous and playful way. By using curriculum drama, students and their teachers will be able to meet defined standards within their social studies unit. Over a decade ago, the National Council for the Social Studies (NCSS) (1994) identified 10 thematic strands that served as the bedrock for social studies curricular standards. Three of these strands are particularly relevant to the curriculum dramas explored within this text:

- Individuals, Groups, and Institutions

Social studies programs should include experiences that provide for the study of *interactions among individuals, groups, and institutions.* (p. 25)

- Power, Authority, and Governance

Social studies programs should include experiences that provide for the study of *how people create and change structures of power, authority, and governance.* (p. 26)

- Civic Ideals and Practices

Social studies programs should include experiences that provide for the study of *the ideals, principles, and practices of citizenship in a democratic republic.* (p. 30)

Whether the curriculum drama is based on the legislative branch of government or on current events, history, or law, this approach reflects serious attention to the power and relevance of NCSS standards. For more information about these curricular standards, please visit the NCSS Web site at http://www.socialstudies.org/standards.

Furthermore, this approach with its emphasis on spoken and written expression and the value it places on doing inquiry and conducting research also integrates key English language arts standards as designed by the International Reading Association (IRA) and the National Council of Teachers of English (NCTE) (1996). Three standards in particular connect to social studies based curriculum dramas:

- Students conduct research on issues and interests by generating ideas and questions and by posing questions.
- Students use a variety of technological and informational resources (e.g., libraries, databases, computer networks, video) to gather and synthesize information and to create and communicate knowledge.
- Students use spoken, written, and visual language to accomplish their own purposes (e.g., for learning, enjoyment, persuasion, and the exchange of information).

For more information on these standards, please visit the NCTE Web site at http://www.ncte.org.

As curriculum drama uses standards from both the NCSS and NCTE, this could be an ideal opportunity for colleagues from different disciplines to work together and join forces to construct with students a common classroom experience.

Emerging From Educational Drama

Curriculum drama is closely aligned to the field of educational drama, where the story emerges from the actions generated by the participants. Influenced by the work of individuals such as Dorothy Heathcote (1984) in Great Britain and Winifred Ward (1957) in the United States, this approach is open-ended, not mimetic in design. Similar to "process drama" (O'Neill, 1995), curriculum drama comes from student and teacher constructions that are loosely based on structures or situations conceived as being fundamental to, or characteristic of, a defined topic of study.

Through the task of constructing a particular frame of reference and collaborating with others through this new context, the individual takes part in building collective belief in a "community in the making" (Greene, 2001). Through this process, the individual explores an entirely new way of being with the world. This connects to how the power of imagination can work alongside the development of identity. Madison (1988) notes,

It is through the imagination, the realm of pure possibility that we freely make ourselves to be who or what we are, that we creatively and imaginatively become who we are, while in the process preserving the freedom and possibility to be yet otherwise than what we have become and merely are. (p. 191)

In this situation, middle school and high school students can go far beyond their adolescent worlds and "set aside familiar distinctions and definitions" (Greene, 1995, p. 3), which can too often typecast an individual in the classroom setting. How often have we heard our students classify themselves or their peers based on test performance, grade point average, or current reading levels? Curriculum drama provides a welcomed break from that restrictive environment. In this emerging community, participants can begin to take notice of who they are; they are given license to envision who they can become. During the course of this experience, they become motivated to take responsibility for their constructed roles and work with the consequences of their collective actions.

Along with participating in the making of a new classroom community, curriculum drama also begins to emulate a "community of practice" (Lave & Wenger, 1991; Wenger, 1998). Students take on the language, engage in the activity, and begin to develop unique perspectives as "insiders" connected to a field of study within social studies. This then provides a steady source of comparison and inspiration between what is happening in the transformed setting of the classroom and what is happening (or happened) in society.

For instance, in the classroom senate, students as senators develop firsthand experience with legislative practice and encounter complex challenges within its process. This then provides them with a useful context to compare their experience in the classroom senate with what is happening within the U.S. Senate. Throughout this drama, they place their experience alongside legislative events happening in society. They explore such questions as the following:

- How does the *structure* of our classroom world compare with that in the adult world?
- How does our *practice* compare with that in the adult world?

Curriculum drama seeks to ensure that the constructed events within the classroom engage student interests and make sense while at the same time serving as bedrock for delving deep within the content of a unit of study. In this way viable points of comparison can be made between the constructed classroom setting and its corresponding context in society.

Why the Term *Curriculum Drama?*

I use the term *curriculum drama* because at its core it is about the lived curriculum. This approach incites student interest and compels their engagement to participate within a defined world within social studies. In so doing, students have the opportunity to develop substantive content understandings. This happens in multiple ways—when students develop a viable frame of reference within this constructed setting, when students *step into* and participate within these contexts, and when students *step away from* the enacted experience to reflect upon an emerging situation and its potential meaning.

At the same time, students apply what they know through their participation in the emerging *drama.* This brings an unpredictable and generative dimension to the teaching and learning environment. It complicates what they know and what they may think they know. At the same time, drama brings out a spirit of playfulness and fun. People become emboldened to imagine the possible and to interact in new ways within its world.

This distinguishes curriculum drama from simulation games where roles and situations are largely predetermined, teacher-directed, and prepackaged. Curriculum drama is more constructivist in its design; students work with one another and their teacher to build their frame of reference, and situations emerge from the activities generated within this context. It is also different from theatrical performances in that there are no scripts. For that matter, value is not placed on "acting" but rather on the ability to contribute in a meaningful and credible way to the conversations and tasks happening within the constructed classroom community.

Summary

This chapter introduces curriculum drama, an innovative approach for constructing social studies contexts within the classroom setting. Participants move from their classroom roles as students to a more dynamic position as engaged insiders within a topic of study. Grounded in actual classroom experiences from a wide range of settings, this approach emerges from the field of educational drama.

What's Next?

The next chapter, "Constructing Curriculum Drama: Exploring Its Structure," examines the inner workings of this classroom approach. Three processes are examined: using a blueprint, setting the stage, and constructing multiple points of entry.

2

Constructing Curriculum Drama

Exploring Its Structure

How do you construct a curriculum drama? What preparations are involved in this work? How do students begin to take part in shaping this classroom experience? This chapter provides a practical guide to help you build a curriculum drama in social studies.

The Inner Workings of Curriculum Drama

Curriculum drama involves both the ongoing construction of curriculum and the building of belief in a new world within the classroom experience. This approach puts into active motion the workings of key concepts, practices, and terminology used within the focus of a given social studies unit. Essentially, this approach has three ongoing and overlapping processes:

- Using a blueprint
- Setting the stage
- Constructing multiple points of entry

When these three processes are working together, the curriculum drama will exert strong motivational pull upon the student to understand and to engage within the driving content of the unit. Each process contributes to a different texture, meaning, and layer within the curriculum drama. The following section describes each of these three processes as its own separate entity. As Figure 2.1 illustrates, however, these processes overlap when interacting within a curriculum drama.

Figure 2.1   Curriculum Drama in Motion

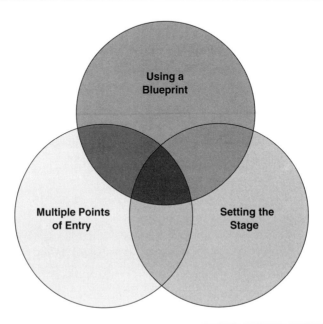

Using a Blueprint

A blueprint informs, but does not necessarily dictate, how a structure will eventually be built. In curriculum drama, a blueprint (or a series of blueprints) organizes the curricular content within the classroom activity. Whether it is civics or history, world cultures or current events, this blueprint is the defining core of the unit of study. As the teacher, I work to identify key blueprints that I can use and manipulate within the curriculum drama. Depending upon the curricular focus, there are a number of resources that can be used as working blueprints. Table 2.1 groups these blueprints in two general categories—a pivotal document and a civic action.

Within the social studies content area that you are teaching, what is (are) the pivotal document(s) that ground(s) your unit of study? What are the common practices, structures, and traditions that connect in some way to this pivotal document? Table 2.2 shows the strategic use of blueprints to frame curriculum drama.

Table 2.1   Types of Blueprints

Pivotal document:	This blueprint serves as the bedrock for the social studies experience.
	Ideas: letter, article, petition (e.g., "Letter from Birmingham Jail," Martin Luther King, Jr., 4/16/1963) key declarations (e.g., Declaration of Independence) governance (e.g., U.S. Constitution) rights of the people (e.g., Bill of Rights) proclamations, resolutions, treaties (e.g., Emancipation Proclamation) acts, laws (e.g., Civil Rights Act of 1964)
Civic action:	This blueprint explores the way publicly elected officials and/or private citizens engage in some form of democratic practice.
	Ideas: building peace deciding justice electing a public official engaging in free speech giving/questioning testimony keeping order making laws reporting the news signing a bill into law taking an oath of office

Table 2.2   Using Blueprints to Frame Curriculum Drama

Content Area	Pivotal Document	Civic Action	Curriculum Drama
Legislative System	U.S. Constitution (Article 1)	Making laws	**Classroom Senate** (see Chapters 3–8)
Current Events	Universal Declaration of Human Rights	Building peace and community	**World Summit on Peace** (see Chapter 9)
History	Declaration of Independence Declaration of Sentiments	Participating in a town hall meeting	**Should Women Vote?** (see Chapter 9)
Judicial System	Bill of Rights (rights of the accused)	Deciding questions of justice	**Criminal Trial** (see Chapter 9)

Teacher Decision Making: Adjusting the Blueprint

Once a defining blueprint has been located, you now need to think about how you could put it into action within the classroom context. Most likely, you will need to make deliberate adjustments based on scheduling realities, availability of resources, and student interests.

For instance, in the legislative drama described in Chapters 3–8, I decided to use as my pivotal document the U.S. Constitution, particularly Article 1, which details the legislative branch of the federal government. Rather than attempt to duplicate the U.S. Congress with its two legislative bodies, the U.S. Senate and House of Representatives, I made the strategic decision to include within the classroom experience only one legislative entity, the senate.

In the making of curriculum drama, there are deliberate adjustments from the original blueprint. This does not mean, however, that student learning is compromised. Throughout the curriculum drama, there is direct emphasis placed on comparing the classroom experience to the topic under inquiry. As inside participants within their own classroom setting (e.g., classroom senate), students are well positioned and well motivated to understand how their experience compares with a similar one in the adult world (e.g., U.S. Congress). The key point here is that content matters; it drives and informs the classroom experience. So in the legislative drama, students use their emerging content understandings and their constructed senate experience as a lens to explore the workings within the U.S. Congress.

Along with adjusting the pivotal document to the classroom experience, you will also need to examine the practices connected to this civic action. For example, within the practice of making laws, the structure of the U.S. Senate presently contains 100 senators. In the classroom context, we reduced that number to 25; this reflected our class size. Table 2.3 details the use of two blueprints and how they were adjusted to guide the preliminary construction of a curriculum drama based on the legislative branch of government.

Student Decision Making: Shaping the Curriculum Drama

Curriculum drama is an approach driven by student participation and engagement, not something that is imposed upon them. While working to frame the curriculum drama with a set of key blueprints, construct openings that will allow students to take part in shaping the direction of the curriculum drama. Identify preliminary decisions that the class could make to participate in the building of this experience.

Table 2.3   Using Blueprints to Construct the Classroom Senate

U.S. Constitution (Pivotal Document)	Making Laws (Civic Action)	Classroom Senate (Curriculum Drama)
All legislative powers herein granted shall be vested in a Congress of the United States, which shall consist of a Senate and House of Representatives. (Article 1, section 1)		• The classroom congress consists of one legislative body, the classroom senate.
The Senate of the United States shall be composed of two senators from each state, for six years; and each senator shall have one vote. (Article 1, section 3)		• One senator per state • Term of office: six weeks
	Structure: The U.S. Senate currently has 100 senators.	• The classroom senate equals the number of students in the class (e.g., 25).
	Tradition: U.S. senators take a formal oath of office.	• Class vote: Students as senators decide whether to take an oath of office.

For instance, in the classroom senate, the students have a series of initial decisions to make. First of all, do they want to construct a senate experience or do they prefer to follow the pages within a textbook? It is their decision, not mine. Inevitably, they choose to construct the classroom experience. Students also face the question about whether they want to be sworn in as senators. Again, it is a student-based decision; as the teacher I am neutral on this point.

> **Looking at Blueprints and Asking Questions**
>
> As you begin to think about how social studies curriculum can transform to a curriculum drama, consider these questions:
>
> Which blueprint can best serve as a framework for grounding the curriculum drama with content?
>
> Which blueprint provides a model for taking civic action and/or building a community of practice?

A well-chosen blueprint can be the inspiration for envisioning a community of practice based on a relevant field of social studies content. This blueprint can guide you in the work of shifting classroom roles (e.g., from student to senator) and envisioning the subsequent activities that the class could engage in within this context (e.g., as legislators making laws). Through this process, students take part in preliminary decision making and become involved in shaping the direction and energizing the momentum of the curriculum drama.

Setting the Stage

Curriculum drama "wakes up" a classroom. Students take notice of one another in new ways, and they become genuinely interested in the content area that is driving the curriculum drama. This approach, however, is not prepackaged. It cannot be hauled out of a closet and "implemented" the following day. Setting the stage for a curriculum drama occurs in the weeks before it becomes an entity within the classroom. Here are some ways to set the stage:

- Setting the tone
- Triggering and sustaining interest
- Using tools of the trade

Setting the Tone

When curriculum drama is in productive motion, the students create their own frame of reference within the setting and participate as inside players within its world. This approach trusts the students to lead and collaborate with one another. If students are overly reliant upon external authority, they will need time to develop skill and experience in social collaboration and peer leadership. In the weeks before constructing a curriculum drama, provide opportunities for students to work in small groups. Hold discussions afterward to reflect upon the experience. What did the students notice in their small group settings (e.g., leadership roles, cooperation)? What did you notice as a classroom teacher? Let the classroom experience act as the "text" for ongoing discussions about student autonomy and responsibility.

Curriculum drama also includes public speaking. Are you ready to hear what the students have to say? Are the students ready to listen respectfully to one another? Are they comfortable and skilled with public speaking? To prepare the class for curriculum drama, provide classroom opportunities for debate and discussion.

Setting the Tone: Classroom Jobs

Classroom jobs are another way to set the stage for curriculum drama. For instance, in preparation for the legislative drama, student jobs can be grouped in committees and can focus on current event issues.

Committee on Urban Affairs:	reports national events
Committee on Foreign Relations:	reports international news
Committee on Culture:	reports on arts and sports
Committee on the Environment:	reports on weather

Triggering and Sustaining Interest

How can the environment work to both trigger and sustain student interest in the curriculum drama? Wall space can be used as a gallery for posting images that relate in some way to the content within the curriculum drama. In the weeks before I plan to initiate a curriculum drama, I scour newspapers, magazines, and calendars, and I cut out images that have some connection to the upcoming unit of study. For instance, in preparation for the classroom senate, I post such visuals as pictures of the U.S. Capitol (interior/exterior), surrounding buildings (e.g., Supreme Court, White House), and news photographs of legislators in action (e.g., giving speeches).

Sparking Interest: Constructing a Public Blog

Post a thought-provoking question that relates in some way to a key concept within your social studies unit. Alongside this question attach a large sheet of blank paper. Include ready access to pencils, pens, or markers. Step aside and in a short while you will have a public blog!

Here are two questions that I have posted as wall blogs. The first triggered our study of American government and the role of democracy in our lives; the second served as an entry point for our legislative unit, and it spurred some students to critically examine federal education laws (e.g., No Child Left Behind Act of 2001).

❑ Is our school a democracy?
❑ What laws should be changed?

Along with creating interest in a given topic, a public blog can also help to build a sense of community. Written responses, whether signed or unsigned, provide a venue for students to thoughtfully and creatively connect with one another and with the curriculum.

Using Tools of the Trade

Just as there are objects that are unique to classroom life (e.g., lesson plan book, attendance record, pencil sharpener), there are "tools of the trade" that help to define other communities of practice. As curriculum drama works to create a new practice and context within the classroom setting, it helps to include these objects within the curriculum drama. Like stepping stones, these objects can entice students to enter into its constructed domain.

For instance, in the legislative drama, when the class decides to hold a full senate session for a debate or vote, the sign "Senate in Session" appears on the classroom door. A senate leader uses a gavel to formally begin the event and to keep order within the session. The lawmakers place their official name cards on their desks, and they refer to one another with the honorific title "Senator." In this instance, the tools of the trade—the senate sign, gavel, desk cards—work together to signal collective entry into our constructed senate event.

Tools of the Trade

Communities of practice often use objects that are unique to their work. As you begin to construct your curriculum drama, cast a wide net to identify items that are commonly encountered in this specialized field.

For instance, in the classroom senate, students have access to these items:

Public records:	U.S. senator's voting record
Objects:	gavel, desk card
Reference sources:	almanac, atlas, national newspapers, U.S. political map.
Signage:	"Senate in Session"
Symbols:	U.S. flag

In addition, students use legislative folders to keep their senate work in order. Inside each folder might be items such as minutes from a senate session, a memo from a committee chairperson, or an agenda for an upcoming regional meeting. Documents of this kind do not typically appear in elementary or secondary school classrooms. By using these particular objects for the legislative context, we are deliberately disrupting what we expect to see in the classroom world. At the same time, these tools of the trade help to foster belief in the classroom's construction of legislative practice.

Multiple Entry Points

Curriculum drama uses several entry points to engage student interest and activity. These entry points include the following:

- Creating situations
- Speaking the language
- Creating coherence in the physical environment

Creating Situations

In curriculum drama, the teacher and students create situations that alter the conventional rhythm of classroom life. In these situations, the class works not as students but as individuals in a constructed event. To prepare for an extended curriculum drama, plan a loose road map of the curricular events that might occur with your students. Of course, once the curriculum drama is set in motion, this initial road map will inevitably change.

For instance, recently I worked as a consultant on a legislative drama with a seventh grade class. Every Friday, the students, teachers, and I constructed situations that built upon the work that had been done within the week. Table 2.4 provides a roadmap of the tasks that students had completed and the Friday events that situated this work within legislative practice.

Students construct their own multidimensional frame of reference within the curriculum drama. They become part of a new web of relationships within the classroom, and they engage in a number of different activities within their constructed positions. In the senate example above, the students constructed their own bills based on state

Table 2.4   Constructing a Road Map: Classroom Senate

Setting the Stage (Week-long projects)	Creating Situations (Friday's session)	For more details see Chapter
Students research the state they will represent in their senate.	Regional conference: Students work in small groups to discuss with colleagues various state, regional, and national issues.	3
Students construct bills.	Senate session: The classroom senate constructs a formal session to recognize each senator's bill and to assign it an official senate number.	6
Students work in committee to prioritize individual bills and/or to construct a committee bill.	Senate vote: Students as senators listen to each committee's prioritized legislation and vote on the bill of top national concern. Senators construct a witness list for next week's hearing.	6
Students review witness testimony and prepare questions for the upcoming hearing.	Senate hearing: Students as senators pose questions to witnesses about their testimony and its connection to the legislation under review.	7
Students prepare speeches for the upcoming debate on the prioritized legislation.	Senate debate: Senators engage in a debate about the benefits and costs of the prioritized legislation.	8

research, regional issues, and personal concerns about society. Working in committee, they prioritized legislation. As a full legislative body, they then voted to determine which of these committee bills to consider first.

Through these multiple entry points, students engage in the practice within the field. Rather than reading a script they are given or playing a required role, students essentially construct and take ownership of their own positions within the curriculum drama. Through informed research and their participatory decisions, the students take an active role in shaping the classroom experience.

Multiple Entry Points: Creating Situations

Curriculum drama uses a variety of situations to create an insider's vantage point within a topic of study. The following lists some constructed events within the legislative drama:

Formal ceremony:	oath of office
Private meeting:	strategy session
Gathering data:	legislative hearing
Amending a bill:	committee session
Taking a stand:	voting on a bill

When the class is engaged, not as students but rather as insiders, it is important that teacher actions and words support and build upon this collective frame of reference. After all, it takes courage and trust for a student to envision and act from a different perspective. Nothing can shatter collective entry into this new world more quickly than an adult's disregard for it. To put it another way, as a teacher you need to do your part to foster belief in this new situation. When a situation emerges where adult authority is called for, think of how you can engage in a strategic and judicious way. Chapters 4–8 include sections on teacher dilemmas and how to work through them.

Speaking the Language

Along with constructing a situation, curriculum drama uses the power of language as another point of entry. Rather than using the day-to-day informal language of the classroom setting, curriculum drama works to incorporate specialized terminology, forms of expression (spoken and written), and speaking protocols. This vocabulary is woven into the classroom experience and is introduced when the students are about to encounter a situation that demands their understanding and use of this language.

For instance, in the legislative drama, I teach the students the rudimentary protocol for engaging in debate. In the days before they engage as senators in this formal experience, they examine the use of such strategic procedures as a filibuster (delivering an extended speech) and voting for cloture (limiting debate). Whether the class decides to use these tactics within their upcoming debate is their decision. For more detail on preparations for the senate debate, see Chapter 8.

Political Terminology: Filibuster and Cloture

Filibuster: This procedural strategy serves to delay action on a bill. A legislator delivers an extended speech, keeping debate in motion while at the same time preventing the bill from moving along in the legislative process.

Cloture: This procedural strategy limits debate, which prevents a filibuster from happening. Three-fifths of the senate needs to vote to approve this measure.

SOURCE: Virtual Reference Desk at http://www.senate.gov

Creating Coherence in the Physical Environment

The physical environment is another point of entry. To what extent does the existing arrangement of furniture help to create belief in constructing a particular community of practice? Can desks and chairs be rearranged in some way so that it becomes a new setting?

For example, in a curriculum drama that is focused on the criminal justice system, I transform the classroom to a courtroom setting. The teacher's desk becomes the judge's bench. On one side of the judge is the witness stand; on the other side is a chair for the bailiff. In addition, on one side of the wall, I arrange space for the jurors to sit. In another area of the room, I place tables for two teams of lawyers.

When used as a supporting structure, the classroom environment can serve as a powerful way to build additional belief and add energy to the curriculum drama. Whether it is a complete room transformation or a more subtle shift with furniture, the students will take notice and reposition themselves within this transformed world. Chapters 3–8 show how, in the legislative drama, the classroom environment can be transformed for different legislative events (e.g., party caucus, hearing, debate).

Occasionally, there may be times when the curriculum drama falters. It happens. Unlike the learning involved in answering chapter questions from a textbook, completing a worksheet, or watching a video, experiential learning is not predictable. It triggers the unexpected. When there is collective disbelief or student resistance, take time to examine these three processes of curriculum drama: using a blueprint, setting the stage, and constructing multiple points of entry. Perhaps one of these processes is out of focus and needs additional attention. Share your concerns with the class, and work with them as collaborators to reinvigorate and build belief back into the emerging curriculum drama.

Summary

This chapter examined the inner workings of curriculum drama. Three processes work to build credibility and momentum within the constructed setting: using a blueprint, setting the stage, and constructing multiple points of entry. While described separately, each constructed process works in concert with the others to build belief in the curriculum drama.

What's Next?

The next chapter, "Becoming a Senator: Setting the Stage," provides detailed strategies for constructing preliminary activities to transform the classroom to create a senate experience. This then provides opportunities for the class to make points of comparison with how the U.S. Senate is organized.

3

Becoming a Senator

Setting the Stage

This chapter explores the process of "setting the stage" for a curriculum drama based on the legislative branch of government. For students to think and interact as senators, a deliberate process takes place that prepares them to take seriously their new positions within the emerging classroom senate. Transformations begin by engaging the class in a number of preliminary activities.

> **Setting the Stage**
>
> *Setting the stage* is an ongoing process between students and their teacher designed to lay the groundwork for the emergent curriculum drama.

Table 3.1 outlines the preliminary tasks, events, and inquiries during this phase of the curriculum drama. Each session runs for about 40 minutes. Depending upon the schedule, it can take between a week and two weeks to complete this phase of the classroom senate. Certain activities include short cuts as well as extensions.

Table 3.1   Plan of Action: Setting the Stage

Topic	Format	Sessions
Starting With a Blueprint: U.S. Constitution	Class meeting	1
Setting the Stage	Class meeting	1
Selecting States for the Classroom Senate	Task	1
Recognizing the Senators	Event	1
Researching States in the Classroom Senate	Task	ongoing
Researching U.S. Senators	Task	2

Classroom Practice: Student Choice

Ask the class whether they want to learn by constructing their own classroom senate or do they want to learn by studying about the legislative branch of government from the pages of a textbook?

    Conduct a public vote! When names are announced, students can stand and either declare

I vote *in favor* of the classroom senate

or

I vote *to oppose* the classroom senate.

A simple majority wins.

Starting With a Blueprint: U.S. Constitution

To ease students into the idea that they will be acting as the legislative branch of government, I first introduce them to the U.S. Constitution. This provides a key blueprint for how the class will construct their senate.

Becoming Familiar With the U.S. Constitution

Have students explore the U.S. Constitution by first paying attention to how it is structured. Many civics books include the document in its entirety. Does yours? Orient the students to how the text of the Constitution separates the power of government into three separate branches of government. Have students locate these sections in the U.S. Constitution:

    Article 1   Legislative Branch

    Article 2   Executive Branch

    Article 3   Judicial Branch

Ask for a volunteer to read Article 1, section 3, clause 3:

The Senate of the United States shall be composed of two senators from each state for six years; and each senator shall have one vote.

Constructing the Classroom Setting

To understand how the classroom senate relates to the U.S. Senate and for that matter to the U.S. Constitution (particularly

Article 1, section 3, clause 3), work with the students to construct a chart. Table 3.2 shows how a class of 25 students compared their ideas for constructing a classroom senate to the existing structure within the U.S. Senate.

In the various classroom senates that I have experienced over the years, one student represents one state. While not all states are represented in the classroom setting, I can work with the students to ensure that at least all regions in the country are represented.

Your Choice: Constructing the Classroom Senate

If students work better in teams, construct the senate by having two senators represent one state. While this will limit the states that are represented in your senate, it will be more closely aligned to the structure outlined within the U.S. Constitution.

As I begin to think about the classroom senate, I am considering the blueprints that I am using and whether I need to adapt or modify them for the classroom experience.

Setting the Stage

Introducing the idea of a classroom senate will undoubtedly stir a range of questions, emotions, and expectations among your students. Pay attention to how children react to this idea. Who seems excited by it? Anxious? Resistant? Would it help if students talked about this

Table 3.2   Points of Comparison: Classroom Senate to U.S. Senate

	Classroom Senate	U.S. Senate
Senators per State	1	2
Total Number of Senators	25	100
States Represented in Senate	25	50
Terms of Office	6 weeks	6 years
Vote	1 person/1 vote	1 person/1 vote

classroom idea in small groups and then wrote about it in their journals? From listening to these small group discussions and reading journal entries, you will be able to gain additional insight into the collective mood of the class.

The Words We Use

The words we speak can convey unintended meanings. For this reason, I use the term "classroom senate" rather than "mock senate" and the "U.S. Senate" rather than the "actual senate." This sends a message to the class that for educational purposes, both settings are real, and both need to be taken seriously.

Extensions: Class Investigations

Art: Have students create a visual image showing the power within the legislative branch of government and how the executive and judicial branches check its power.

Current events: Have students locate news articles and images that show the interaction between and among these three branches of government.

Geographic inquiry: On a street map of Washington, D.C., have students locate the notable buildings that house these three branches of government (i.e., Congress, White House, Supreme Court).

Historical inquiry: Did the U.S. Senate always represent 50 states? By looking at the signatures on the U.S. Constitution and identifying the states the signers were from, students will have clues about the preliminary composition of the first U.S. Senate.

Student inquiry: If you had a choice to work in one of the branches of government, which branch would you choose? Compare the salary of a supreme court justice with that of the U.S. president and a member of Congress. Why are their salaries part of the public record?

Selecting States for the Classroom Senate

Determine which states should be represented in the classroom senate. Include states that reflect a range of geographic regions, physical sizes, demographics, and political stances. For one classroom senate, the students and I used the following list of regions to make sure that all areas of the United States were represented:

- Pacific Coast
- Rocky Mountains

- Southwest
- Great Plains
- Midwest
- South
- Northeast

Once you and/or the students have constructed a list of potential states for the classroom senate, you need to determine how the students will select the state they will represent in this legislative experience. Depending upon the length of your class period, this can be done in a single session or as an extended experience.

Single Session Experience

The following two strategies provide a straightforward way for determining which student will represent which state. One relies on chance; the other relies on a combination of luck and choice.

Chance

On folded pieces of paper, write the name of each state chosen for the classroom senate. Have students randomly make a selection. The name written on the paper will be that individual's state. After each piece of paper is drawn, students can write their names next to their states on the posted senate list or on a wall map of the United States.

> **Optional Idea**
>
> After states have been determined by either chance or choice, consider providing time for students to engage in a round of peer negotiations. For those who are disappointed in representing particular states, offer them the opportunity to trade. Provide a defined time frame for this activity.
>
> In the event of a potential state switch, all interested parties must be amenable to the agreement.

Choice

Rather than writing the names of the states on pieces of folded paper, write numbers instead. Have each student randomly select a folded paper. After all the pieces of paper have been drawn, ask who has the number 1. This individual is now the first to select a state. The student who has number 2 goes next. Proceed until everyone has selected a state. To keep track of which states have been "claimed," have students write their names next to their selected states on a prominent class list.

Extended Series of Sessions

Provide classroom time to explore maps, almanacs, tourist brochures, and national statistics on each state (e.g., high school graduation rates, crime statistics). Afterward, each student could identify three state choices. While they will be able to choose only one state to represent in the classroom senate, the other two will serve as backups if they do not get their first choice.

For homework or as a class writing assignment, have students explore their reasons for selecting these states.

Constructed Senate: Varied Reasons for Selecting a State

As can be seen from the following student reflections from one senate experience, individuals selected states for a variety of reasons:

❑ The state that I would like to represent most is Montana. . . . I don't know much about it, but I like the fact that it has no speed limits, and I've seen it in movies and it is very beautiful. (Stan)

❑ I know New York. I'm used to it and wouldn't want to live anywhere else. (Katie)

Collect student choices and aggregate these data yourself. For those who want their first choice and are vying with others for the same state, provide time for peer negotiations. Students need to be ready to fall back on alternative choices—like going with either their second or third choice. Perhaps they might also consider a state from the same geographic region as their first choice.

Strategically, the more students are able to position themselves as having a personal connection with a particular state (e.g., family ties), or the deeper their understanding about a particular region in the country, the more likely they will be to have a successful outcome in their negotiations with peers.

Of course, peer negotiations do not always work. When this occurs, be prepared to get directly involved. In the spirit of mutual problem solving, advise students to consider alternative states or regions. When entrenched positions are taken, and negotiations have stalled, invite the students to decide by lottery. Competing

Peer Negotiations Can Take Time

A variety of strategies can be used to resolve the dilemma of people wanting the same first choice. Concentrate first on less complicated negotiations (i.e., two students seeking the same state), and gradually work on those popular states where there are a number of hopeful candidates.

students can place their names in a hat, and the person whose name is drawn will then be the senator for that contested state.

Teacher Role in State Selection Process

The more you can use your authority to facilitate, and not dictate, the outcome of this process, the more likely your students will be to take ownership of this experience. As each senator has one vote, it does not matter in the long run who represents which state. What is important is that students take ownership of their responsibility as a senator in representing their constituents' interests and concerns.

Wall Display

Post a large wall map of the United States in the classroom. Upon conclusion of successful peer negotiations, students can post their names on their respective states. Rather than having them identify themselves informally with their first names, have each student write "Senator" followed by his or her full name.

For those who remain in negotiations about which state they will represent, the map provides a visual image of those states and regions that still need representation.

Teachable Moment: Points of Comparison

The process of state selection provides an ideal opportunity to investigate the constitutional requirements for becoming a U.S. senator. Have students read the following section in the U.S. Constitution:

No person shall be a Senator who shall not have attained to the age of thirty years, and been nine years a citizen of the United States, and who shall not, when elected, be an inhabitant of that State for which he shall be chosen. (Article 1, section 3, clause 3)

Table 3.3 shows a chart comparing senator qualifications in the classroom senate and in the U.S. Senate.

Table 3.3   Points of Comparison: Senator Qualifications

	Classroom Senate	U.S. Senate
Age	?	30 years or older
U.S. Citizenship	?	citizen for at least 9 years
Resident of the State	?	yes

Classroom Choice: Requirements for Students as Senators

How can you adapt the requirements of being a U.S. senator to the realities of the classroom senate? Here are some ideas:

Age: How old is the youngest person in the class? That number could be the official minimum age for the senators in the classroom senate.

Citizenship: Rather than U.S. citizenship (you may have undocumented students), the senate could have students who are simply members of the class.

Resident of the state: Rather than being a resident of a defined state, the student as senator agrees to conduct research on his/her state.

Recognizing the Senators: An Event

Once everyone is settled on a state, construct a simple classroom event or formal ceremony that acknowledges the students' new status as senators. In this way, there is communal recognition and a building of collective belief to how the classroom is transforming to a senate.

Unlike the president, who is required by the Constitution to take a specific oath upon beginning the duties of the office (Article 2, section 1, clause 8), U.S. senators take an oath based on internal U.S. Senate rules and tradition. Since 1862, U.S. senators publicly state and in writing confirm the following oath of office:

> I do solemnly swear (or affirm) that I will support and defend the Constitution of the United States against all enemies, foreign and domestic; that I will bear true faith and allegiance to the same; that I take this obligation freely, without any mental reservation or purpose of evasion; and that I will well and faithfully discharge the duties of the office on which I am about to enter: So help me God. (United States Senate, n.d.)

If the class decides to follow existing U.S. Senate practice, students can sign the official document shown in Resource A and keep it as a memento.

Alternative to Taking an Oath of Office

Rather than take a formal oath of office, students could simply be recognized for their new positions as senators. In one senate experience, I worked as "senate clerk" and announced the following to the class:

> By the power vested in me as senate clerk (*I paused, smiling; students looked quizzically at each other*), I will now formally announce each state and its senator. I will proceed in alphabetical order by state.

- From the great state of **Alaska** (bolded for vocal emphasis), we have Senator Leah Brown. (*Senator Brown spontaneously stands up and the class applauds.*)
- From the great state of **Colorado,** we have Senator Jim Cape. (*Senator Cape remains seated and waves in response to peer applause*). . . .

A constructed ceremony, whether it is staged formally or casually, marks an important classroom moment in curriculum drama. It provides a break from the ordinary. In addition, it can pull the group together as they interact as participants within this experience. Such a ceremony can also be the ideal jumping off point from which to examine the nature and contexts of civic oaths in society (e.g., the jury's oath and witness oaths in criminal trials).

Constructed Senate: Whose State Is the Best?

Directly after the induction ceremony, the topic "Whose state is the best?" became the prevailing topic of peer-directed conversations in my classroom. Students began to search through almanacs, tourist brochures, and national statistics to learn more about their states and geographic regions. Rather than taking on the "mantle of the expert" role (Heathcote & Herbert, 1985), students became more like independent inquirers. They informally researched their states in part because they wanted to participate in this current classroom situation.

While the competitive nature of this conversation did not necessarily convey senatorial propriety, it did reveal how students took personal interest and pride in their emerging presence within the classroom senate. Students shared data that positioned their states in a favorable context (e.g., high rate of high school graduation). Sometimes a student used national statistics to reveal critical aspects of other states (e.g., unemployment rates).

Researching the States in the Classroom Senate

Once the class has settled on the states they plan to represent in the senate, and individuals have begun to do informal investigations of their own states, assign an extended state research report. By investigating the geography, demographics, and current issues facing their respective states, students will be better informed about their work. During the course of a two week time span, students can use a variety of materials for this independent project, including such reference sources as encyclopedias, almanacs, atlases, and Web sites like http://www.senate.gov and http://www.50states.com. Resource B contains guidelines for these research reports.

Let the library staff know ahead of time about this project. They may be able to recommend and/or reserve key resources for this task. Parents and caregivers will also appreciate knowing about this project and how they can help.

Extension: Talking About Research Before Doing It

Before students engage in their state research projects, hold a class meeting to explore their prior experiences with research assignments. In the sharing of research memories, students will have the opportunity to reflect upon their own patterns of work and to examine their peers' reported background in this area. Here are prompts to trigger discussion:

- ❑ What research projects have you done before?
- ❑ What has been your experience with gathering material? Organizing notes? Meeting project deadlines?
- ❑ What suggestions do you have for one another or for the teacher to ensure a successful experience during this research process?

This conversation is also valuable in that it allows you, the teacher, to get a read on students and how they plan to approach this assignment. In this way, you can consider how best to support and challenge the students in this work.

Here are ways to differentiate the assignment for different learning needs:

- For those who appeared to have a pattern of missing project deadlines, create staggered deadlines on parts of their work.

- For those who reported difficulty with gathering and organizing notes, have the students experiment with various graphic organizers (e.g., outline form, webbing).
- Encourage those who recognized their tendency to become unfocused while gathering data to set time limits while approaching this research task. They might also benefit from having a set of defined research questions in front of them, as they begin to take notes.
- Some students might benefit more by writing down talking points about their states than by completing a full scale research report.

Extension: Applying State Research to a Regional Conference

If time is on your side, arrange for your students to meet in a "regional conference" with their neighboring colleagues. In clusters of 3 to 6, students could informally share findings from their state research work.

Vicky, representing a state from the Midwestern region, noted the following after a session in her regional conference:

I thought it was interesting how almost every state in the Midwest was having financial problems. I did not understand how these problems could be related to one area. But then I was informed that a lot of car plants were centered in that area and they were laying off workers.

Setting the stage for curriculum drama takes time. It is not something that can be done overnight. Students need to become comfortable with their new positions, and they need time to develop content understandings about what they are expected to know. In the context of the legislative drama, the more the students understand their states and regions, the more they will be able to participate in an informed and effective way within the senate.

Interdisciplinary Extension: Research and Map Making

Have students gather by region. Students can work together to first create a large wall map that outlines the states within each particular region. Each group can then determine the thematic map they wish to create. After conducting research and constructing a map legend, each group can plot one of the following details on their map:

(Continued)

(Continued)

Topography: major rivers, mountain ranges

Infrastructure: highways, railroads, airports

Landmarks: historical sites, universities

Hot topics: nuclear waste sites, prisons

Paints can add an aesthetic dimension to this project.

Researching U.S. Senators

At the same time that they are conducting state research, students can also explore the public records of their U.S. senators. This exploration will help their state research. By navigating through http://www.senate.gov, they will be able to obtain the following information:

- Visual image of the senator
- Legislative initiatives
- Committee assignments
- Recorded vote on recent legislation

Another Web site to explore is http://bioguide.congress.gov. This provides biographical information on current and former members of Congress. Each biography contains such information as the following:

- Birth date and place
- Education
- Military service
- Previous career experience
- Political party
- Publications
- Resource C contains a sample worksheet designed to compare the senators from a given state.

Extension: Inquiry Into U.S. Senators

Time permitting, have students survey the class to determine patterns from the public record of their U.S. senators. Here are some lines of inquiry to get started:

Politics: Which states have U.S. senators who are both from the same political parties? From different political parties?

Previous career: What is the most common career that U.S. senators have had before they became senators?

Military service: What percentage of our U.S. senators have served in the military?

Key votes: Who voted for or opposed a key bill in the last Congress? (To answer this question, students can go to http://www.senate.gov → Legislation and Records [top bar] → Votes [side bar].)

When students access these Web sites and engage in varied lines of investigation, the U.S. Senate will become a bit more personalized for them. For instance, looking at the images posted on the official Web sites of their U.S. senators, students will realize that there are actual people involved in this elected office. The U.S. Senate will also become a bit more complicated for them through this line of inquiry. For instance, just because two U.S. senators may represent the same state does not mean that they are in the same committees, share the same politics, or vote the same way on legislative issues.

Constructed Senate: Who Are We as Senators?

While investigating the public record of U.S. senators, the students in one of my classes became concerned. Some thought they would have to take on the political stance of one of their senators and mimic the way that official voted on legislative issues.

I reminded the class that this investigation was simply a way for them to find out more about their chosen states and their own roles as senators. I reassured them that they would go beyond simply copying the position of their current U.S. senators. Instead, students as senators will determine their *own* positions on political issues and construct their *own* legislative initiatives.

Limited Computer Access?

A favorite resource of mine is *The Almanac of American Politics* published by the National Journal Group in Washington, D.C. (Barone & Cohen, 2007). Investigate whether your town or school library has a recent edition of this book, or purchase it for your own class library.

The text is divided according to the 50 states and also includes the four U.S. territories (Puerto Rico, Virgin Islands, Guam, and

American Samoa). Each section contains an essay describing the geography, history, and current issues of the state or territory. This is followed by a section on the state's governor and elected officials in the U.S. Senate and House of Representatives. An excerpt from the profile of Senator Barbara Boxer, junior senator from California is provided in Table 3.4.

As can be seen from this excerpt, profile data on U.S. senators includes such information as the following:

- Educational background
- Professional career
- Committee work
- Ratings on various issues
- Public voting record on key legislative issues

Before students explore their U.S. senators' profile data, it might be helpful to first orient the class to one individual's record. What meanings do students make from these data? Afterward, distribute profiles on students' two U.S. senators. What does the class notice about the career background, committee work, and/or voting record of these two individuals?

Investigating the public record of our elected officials through numerous data sources is a valuable and an eye-opening experience for students. Through this work, students begin to glimpse the personal background behind the public image of legislators.

Summary

This chapter explored the intricate process of setting the stage for a curriculum drama. As part of this coconstruction process, the U.S. Constitution, particularly Article 1, was used as a primary blueprint for the design of the classroom senate. Students began to gain entry into the world of the senate by first conducting state research. Students became motivated in learning more, not because of the extrinsic threat of an upcoming test, but rather from a more self-interested source. They wanted to be well informed so as to participate in an active and credible way within this new context.

At the same time, students took notice of how their classroom senate compared to the existing structure within the U.S. Senate. Through comparisons between these two settings, content was being introduced, explored, and reinforced.

Table 3.4   Data Profile of a U.S. Senator

**California: Junior Senator
Barbara Boxer (D)**

Committees

- Commerce, Science & Transportation
  (5th of 12 D) Oceans, Atmosphere,
  Fisheries & Coast Guard; Aviation
  Operations, Safety & Security;
  Interstate Commerce, Trade &
  Tourism; Science, Technology &
  Innovation.

- Environment & Public Works (Chmn.
  of 10 D) Public Sector Solutions to
  Global Warming, Oversight &
  Children's Health Protection (Chmn.).

- Ethics (Select) (Chmn. of 3 D).

- Foreign Relations (5th of 11 D) East
  Asian & Pacific Affairs (Chmn.);
  International Development & Foreign
  Assistance, Economic Affairs &
  International Environmental
  Protection; Near Eastern & South &
  Central Asian Affairs.

Barbara Boxer (D)
Elected 1992, 3d full term up 2010

Born:	11-11-1940, Brooklyn, NY
Home:	Rancho Mirage
Education:	Brooklyn Col., B.A. 1962
Religion:	Jewish
Marital Status:	married (Stewart)
Elected Office:	Marin Cnty. Bd. of Supervisors, 1976–82; U.S. House of Reps., 1982–92
Professional Career:	Stockbroker & researcher, 1962–65; Journalist, Pacific Sun, 1972–74; Dist. aide, U.S. Rep. John Burton, 1974–76
DC Office:	112 HSOB, 20510 202-224-3553 Fax: 415-956-6700 Web site: boxer.senate.gov
State Offices:	Fresno: 559-497-5109; Los Angeles: 213-894-5000; Sacramento: 916-448-2787; San Bernardino: 909-888-8525; San Diego: 619-239-3884; San Francisco: 415-403-0100

National Journal Ratings:

	2006 LIB	—	2006 CONS
Economic	87%	-	0%
Social	92%	-	7%
Foreign	98%	-	0%

Key votes of the 109th Congress:

1. Bar ANWR Drilling	Y	5. Confirm Samuel Alito N	9. Limit Interstate N
2. FY06 Spending Curb	N	6. Path to Citizenship Y	Abortion
3. Estate Tax Repeal	N	7. Bar Same Sex N	10. CAFTA N
4. Raise Minimum Wage	Y	Marriage	11. Urge Iraq Withdrawal Y
		8. Stem Cell Research $ Y	12. Provide Detainee Rights Y

SOURCE: Barone, M., & Cohen, R. (2007). *The Almanac of American Politics.* Washington, D.C.: National Journal Group, p. 161.

What's Next?

Chapter 4 examines the building of belief in the classroom senate. Students become aligned to groups called either "Republican" or "Democrat." To develop an affiliation to their party, they collaborate to shape a political agenda that begins to reflect their group's legislative priorities. This then provides the impetus to compare political platforms—those constructed within the classroom senate, and those within the U.S. Senate.

4

Political Parties

Building Belief

Curriculum drama creates an opportunity for students to develop complex understandings of content, while at the same time it seeks to build a learning environment where students are situated in a particular frame of reference. The previous chapter described the process of setting the stage where students became aligned to a particular state and developed insight about their U.S. senators by researching public voting records.

This chapter and the one following it are focused on developing the political landscape of the classroom senate. These two chapters take a detour from the law-making activity of Congress. Depending upon your intended goals and your available time frame, you may decide to skim these two chapters for background purposes only and proceed to Chapter 6, where students construct legislation.

In the activities covered in this chapter, students divide into teams designated as "Republican" or "Democrat." In these groups, they devise political agendas that represent their unique position as participating members of that party. Table 4.1 outlines the preliminary plan of action for this phase of the classroom senate.

The final segment of this chapter is entitled "Classroom Dilemma: Encountering Disbelief." Using a situation from my own classroom experience, I recount a time when a group of students became distracted from senate activity. Rather than grapple seriously with their task, they detached from the legislative world and plunged into bouts of laughter. This section describes how as a teacher I worked to build credibility back into the senate experience.

Table 4.1   Plan of Action: Building a Political Context

Topic	Situation	Session
Consulting With a Blueprint—U.S. Senate	Class work	1
Setting the Stage Perceptions of political parties Published documents	Class work	2
Creating Political Affiliations	Teacher task	
Recognizing Political Groups	Event	1
Constructing a Political Agenda	Group work	2

Classroom Practice: Doing Social Studies

Rather than *studying about* a topic, work alongside students to construct a situation where they can *interact within* the unit of study. This chapter provides ideas for constructing two political entities within the classroom structure, so that students can begin to understand the nature of partisan politics.

Consulting With a Blueprint: U.S. Senate

As a class, investigate the political membership within the current U.S. Senate. Go to http://www.senate.gov for this data. How many are Republicans? Democrats? Which party is currently in the majority?

What should be the comparable ratio of "Republicans" and Democrats" in the classroom senate? Aligning the classroom senate to the current political ratio within the U.S. Senate provides a ready point of comparison between these two settings. Without deciding who should be in which group, have the class determine the number of Democrats and Republicans in the classroom senate.

$$\frac{\text{number of students as senators in the Democratic group}}{\text{number of students in classroom senate}} = \frac{\text{number of U.S. senators in the Democratic party}}{100 \text{ (number of U.S. senators)}}$$

This experience places students on notice that the structure of the classroom senate will have an added dimension to it. Along with representing the interests of their state and region, students as senators will soon belong to a Republican or Democratic group. Depending upon whether they are in the majority or not, students will also have the opportunity to experience the complexity of power and engage in political strategy. This moves the senate experience from being an individual experience—researching one's state, investigating one's U.S. senators—to a more peer-oriented experience where students construct and direct their group's political agenda.

> **Extension: Discussion Questions**
>
> What is the difference, if any, between an elected public official who serves the interests of American citizens and one who follows the political agenda of his or her party?
> What is the relationship, if any, between political parties and the democratic process?

Setting the Stage

In a democracy, citizens have the right to access independent sources of information (Dahl, 2003). Books and Web sites are one source of information. People are another. The following activity provides students with the opportunity to question receptive neighbors and family members about their impressions of political parties.

Perceptions of Political Parties

For homework, have students pose the following two questions to a few adults. Rather than summarizing their responses, have the student bring in exact quotes.

- What is a Republican?
- What is a Democrat?

On separate sheets of poster paper labeled "Republican" or "Democrat," record the class data as the students report their findings. Use a blue marker to list the data on Democrats and a red marker for Republican data; this could then lead into a discussion about "blue states" and "red states."

In your role as scribe, simply record this information. You are not determining what is correct or inaccurate. The point to this activity is to make visible the popular perceptions about these two parties. At a later point, refer back to these data to make points of clarification.

This activity generates comparative observations and preliminary analyses about our two major political parties. It also makes visible those areas that need to be addressed in further depth. For instance, as my students were steeped in liberal politics from their families' backgrounds and neighborhoods, it was evident that they knew more about the Democratic Party than they did about the Republican Party. As their teacher, I needed to address this discrepancy. Nonetheless, this activity did provide basic information on both parties about the following areas:

- Political leaders (past and present)
- Issues of national concern
- Political symbols (elephant/donkey)

Constructed Senate: Gathering Data on Public Perception of Political Parties

Students in my class gathered data on Republicans and Democrats by first asking adults their impressions of what these terms meant. I ("Catherine") began the session, by posing the following question:

Catherine: What quotes do you have about Democrats?

Stan: My dad said that "Democrats believe that it is the government's responsibility to try to solve social policy and problems."

Abigail: My mother told me that "Democrats tend to raise taxes. . . ."

Catherine: What about the Republicans?

Mary: My older sister e-mailed me the following: "Republicans believe that individuals have the right to make basic decisions about how to live their lives without government interference."

Brian: My neighbor read somewhere that "Republicans will cut federal programs, rather than raise taxes. . . ."

Published Documents

As a follow-up assignment, have students investigate the published policy statements from the national committees of these two parties. What do they notice about these documents? How are they similar? Different?

Democratic National Committee: http://www.democrats.org

Republican National Committee: http://www.gop.com

Shortcut

Skim the above Web sites ahead of time and locate common themes. To what extent do these political organizations offer multiple ways for addressing national issues?

For another task, have students go to http://www.senate.gov to determine the political affiliation of their own U.S. senators. Survey the class to determine which states have U.S. senators who are both Democrats or both Republicans. Which students have senators who belong to different parties? Resource D contains a related activity sheet that students can use.

> **An Idea: Going Beyond Mainstream Parties**
>
> Have students go beyond the two mainstream parties and explore the platforms of other political coalitions (e.g., Green Party). This might give them ideas for issues they could include in their own parties' political agendas.

Creating Political Affiliations

Announce to the class that they will be placed into one of two groups. One group will be named "Democrats" and the other group will be named "Republicans." Be transparent about this process with the students. Use the political affiliations of the students' U.S. senators as a guide to determine which party to assign to each individual senator.

For instance, if a student's state has two U.S. senators who are Democrats, then as a senator that student would be placed with the group called the Democrats. If a student's state has two U.S. senators who are Republicans, then as a senator that student would be placed with the Republican group. Students whose states have U.S. senators who belong to different parties—one a Republican, the other a Democrat—should be tentatively placed in one of the two groups. After considering gender balance, group dynamics, and the ratio of Democrats to Republicans, make final decisions about who belongs to which group.

Recognizing Political Groups: An Event

Remind students that regardless of the group name, Republican or Democrat, **they will define their own political party**. Neither group has to follow a preexisting platform. They can if they want become the *new* Democrats or the *new* Republicans. Or if they choose, they can emulate the prevailing political stance of their respective parties. The decision is theirs.

Constructed Senate: Announcing the Republicans and Democrats of the Classroom Senate

While students may already have an idea of which political group they will be assigned to based on the party that their U.S. senators are connected to, the formal announcement makes it official. At the time we did our legislative unit, the U.S. Senate had a Republican majority.

Upon getting the class's attention, I announced:

By the power vested in me as senate clerk, I will now formally announce the members within each of the political parties of our senate (*sustained pause to increase dramatic tension*). The Republicans, being currently in the majority, will be announced first, followed by those who are Democrats (*partial pause*). I will proceed alphabetically, by the senator's last name.

The Republicans are Senator Leah Brown, Senator Jim Cape.

The Democrats are Senator William Belt, Senator Jill Fox.

To mark this defining event, construct a chart with the state and political affiliation of each senator in your class. Distribute it to the class and post it in a visible display. Students will enjoy seeing themselves listed as "Senator," and it provides a way for keeping track of everyone's respective frame of reference within the classroom senate (see Resource E).

Constructing a Political Agenda

Divide the class into two groups along party lines. See Figure 4.1 for room arrangement for members of the majority party. Those in the minority party could assemble in a quiet, supervised corner of the hallway.

Each student-run party now faces the task of constructing a political agenda. To set the stage for this endeavor, have them engage in a series of preparatory activities within their groups. These experiences will help to build a viable dynamic and will further develop their content understandings about existing political agendas in the two major parties.

Students are not expected to mimic or adopt current political ideologies. Rather, they are encouraged to construct their own approach to being Democrats or being Republicans. If they want to, they could use their earlier study of political parties as a frame of reference to advocate becoming *new* Democrats or *new* Republicans.

For the teacher, this is a defining moment. Divided into two self-contained groups, the students—not the teacher—are the ones who are now determining their parties' political directions and agendas.

Figure 4.1 Party Caucus: Classroom Arrangement

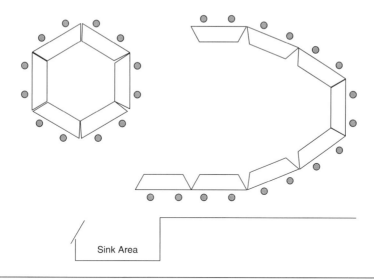

Sink Area

As a result, the teacher-student interactions change. The teacher supports the students to develop a productive work environment within their respective groups. Along with observing the group process, the teacher listens to the students so as to keep updated with the progress made within their work sessions.

Political Terminology: Caucus

When students hear the word "party," they often think "fiesta." It might be prudent to discuss the meaning of this term before they meet.

Caucus: This word means to "meet together." It comes originally from the Algonquian language, a language spoken by native people from various tribes in the Northeast region of North America.

Party Caucus: This is an informal meeting by a political party to discuss and explore topics of concern.

SOURCE: Virtual Reference Desk at http://www.senate.gov

Party Caucus 1: Getting to Know One's Colleagues

Arrange for students to meet in their respective political groups. Have students share what they know about their states and the issues facing their regions. Students could also share what they know about their two U.S. senators (e.g., public voting record). Their group conversations may form the basis for identifying key issues that they will want to address within their parties.

An Idea: Creating Separate Meeting Space for Party Caucus Sessions

To further develop the sense that there are separate political parties, have the two groups in the classroom senate meet in different areas of the school. Could the majority party meet in the classroom, and those in the minority party meet in the hallway? In this way, each group could develop its own agenda and process without being distracted by the other group. At the same time, this separate meeting arrangement can further the sense of belief and purpose in being a member of an autonomous unit.

As the teacher, you will need to move back and forth between these two meeting spaces to observe their progress and/or challenges.

Party Caucus 2: Exploring Existing Political Agendas

For homework, or as an in-class research assignment, have students find out about their respective parties' agendas in the U.S. Senate. These Web sites are helpful:

U.S. Senate Democrats: http://democrats.senate.gov

U.S. Senate Republicans: http://republican.senate.gov

In their second party caucus, have students begin to discuss ideas for forming each party's platform. They can do this by first exploring the following questions:

- What topics were highlighted within their party's senate site?
- From these listed topics, which ones are most important to the members of the Democrat group? The Republican group?
- What topics were not highlighted within this Web site but should have been?
- What are the slogans (rhetoric) used within each party?

Political Terminology: Party Platform

Before students begin their work on a party platform, they need to know the meaning of this term. Otherwise, they might think it is a platform on which to party!

Party Platform: This is the collective set of basic views, aims, and priorities of a political party.

SOURCE: Virtual Reference Desk at http://www.senate.gov

Shortcut

Identify three prevailing topics of national concern that will appeal to the interests of the class (e.g., education, environment, health care). Have each group discuss and then write a general statement that provides big ideas in how to address some aspect of these issues. Resource F contains a sample form for constructing a party platform.

Student Samples

As I had done the classroom senate for a number of years, I had several samples of party platforms accumulated. I provided these as a resource to a classroom senate. These documents fueled ideas for the fledgling senators. It helped both parties to jumpstart their political agendas.

Party Plank: Education

Both the Democratic and Republican groups placed education as a key priority in their respective party platforms.

Democratic Group: Every American family deserves an educational system designed to fully educate their children for the twenty-first century. We support the strengthening of public schools in this country. We plan to do this in part by requiring art classes, second language instruction, and physical education. Schools need to support the whole child's development.

Republican Group: Schools need to be accountable to the American taxpayers. Standardized tests provide an objective way to keep track of a school's yearly academic progress. In this way, the government can alert those schools that are not reaching required standards and expectations.

Student Constructions: Expecting the Unexpected

What do you do when a group of students seeks to place a potentially divisive issue on their party's platform? Will this derail the legislative unit? This has not been my experience. In fact, it usually becomes a teachable moment. We only need to examine our nation's history to understand how conventional ideas were once considered controversial (e.g., women's suffrage, civil rights). As educators we need to trust our students *and* the democratic process happening within our classroom.

When unexpected developments occur, consider becoming a political consultant! In the particular instance of creating a party platform, remind members who represent special interests of their need to gather majority support for the issue to be placed on their party's official platform statement. If the idea does not get needed traction within their own party, encourage them to lobby their colleagues in the other party. If this does not work, help them to think of alternative ideas (e.g., stage a "press conference").

Each year the classroom senate distinguishes itself from its predecessors. Sometimes, the senate constructs defined agendas; one group promotes a more liberal approach, while another supports a more conservative one. Other years, the senate might be more centrist; both parties have similar moderate approaches to the same issues.

Ultimately, the senate depends upon student choice and decision making, not on expected mandates. Whether the two groups decide to construct their parties' platforms in similar or in distinct ways, the process provides students with an ideal opportunity to compare their own platform statements with those published by their parties' respective national committees. Recommend that the Republican group explore http://www.gop.com and the Democratic group explore http://www.democrats.org.

Classroom Dilemma: Encountering Disbelief

Curriculum drama demands collective belief in the possible. This section explores how a group of students and I encountered disbelief and how we worked together to reset the stage for the classroom senate. As seen in the following dialogue, when the "Republicans" first met, they were challenged by the idea that they were now representing this political group in the classroom senate.

Struggles in Developing a Republican Platform

Thirteen students began work to determine their party's political agenda. Although they were "Republicans" in their classroom senate, most considered themselves as being Democrats in real life.

Stan:	Are we going to change our views on things? Because most of us are Democrats.
Jim:	Well, I think that a lot of people think that Republicans don't care about poor people.
Alex:	(*interjecting*) **That's stereotyping** (*bolded for spoken emphasis*).

Jim:	No Alex, that is not what we should be like, but what I think a lot of people think they are like.
Amanda:	(*calling out*) like Democrats!
Leah:	(*in response to Amanda*) I don't think that the Republicans. . . .
Stan:	(*interrupting*) We **are** (*bolded for spoken emphasis*) the Republicans.
Leah:	What I am saying is that practically everyone here is a Democrat.
Jorge:	(*dramatically crying out*) No!
Alex:	(*shouting*) **No! No!** (*spoken emphasis*)
Stan:	We are all Republicans. Right now we are in Washington, D.C. (*The group erupts into laughter.*)

The first Republican caucus showed the raw struggle of a group involved in the social process of building collective meaning and working to create a common frame of reference. Most had concerns about being assigned to this party; it contradicted their personal views of themselves—as Democrats. Stan faced this challenge directly by questioning whether the group should simply change their liberal views and adopt conservative ideology. ("Are we going to change our views on things?") During this situation, the group recognized the sharp disconnect between the classroom senate and the U.S. Senate. Stan's humorous remark was on the mark; they were not Republicans and they were not in Washington, D.C.

> ### Stepping In Versus Breaking From
>
> *Stepping in* refers to those times when there is a collective willingness to interact within a defined frame of reference (e.g., as senators) in the transformed classroom world.
>
> *Breaking from* refers to a situation when there are credibility issues at stake, and the group collectively distances itself from the curriculum drama.

Rather than *stepping in* to engage in discussion about how to think about their political party, students *broke from* the situation entirely. At that moment, the drama had lost its credibility.

Teacher Dilemma

As painful as it was to witness group struggles, I remained for some time in the room listening and taking notes on the group's interactions. From a short distance away, I glumly sat and wondered what to do. My first impulse was to intervene. Isn't that our practice when groups become unfocused?

By doing nothing, I worried that I was sending an unintended message that all was well. In fact, it was just the opposite. All was not well. I observed people interrupting and not listening to one another. I remained silent a bit longer and continued to think how best to handle the situation.

How could I intervene in this situation? I was in a new role now as "observer." I even had a tag on my jacket that identified me in this position. If I used my adult authority to break from this role, I ran the risk of undermining the group's attempts to work through their challenge. Wasn't the whole purpose of this experience to grapple with the idea of what it means to be aligned to a political context?

Still it was clear from the physical arrangement of the room that something was not right. Rather than 13 seats being arranged in a formation where all could be seen or heard, students in some desks blocked the view of others. A few students were seated off to the side away from the main group; at times they engaged in private conversations with each other. The main group did not appear to include everyone in their discussion.

I continued to avert my eyes from the group and to think how best to handle the situation. Laughter lingered a while longer. Eventually, someone had an idea.

Constructed Senate: Beginning Steps to Develop a Republican Agenda

Eli sat away from the main group listening to the flow of conversation. At one point, the laughter died down, and he stated,

We shouldn't think of ourselves as Democrats or Republicans. I think we are not old enough to know about these views. I think we should just have our views and not be Democrats or Republicans.

Eli began to refocus the group. By emphasizing the importance of "having our views," he urged the group to break out of the fixed boundaries of political labels. The group did not have to change their personal views and pretend that they were something they were not. Instead, as Eli reminded them, they could stay true to their own views. The group began to take notice of this idea and they stepped back into their task.

It took time, humor, and thought for these students to coalesce under this term "Republican." They had to move from viewing this term from the third person "they" to the more familiar view that it was now "we." Heathcote referred to this as "feeling on the inside" (Wagner, 1976, p. 78). Students had to work though their sense of disequilibrium. They needed time to come up with "big ideas" (Schifter & Fosnot, 1993) about being "Republican," when as Leah said, "Practically everyone here is a Democrat." They had to "break set with old assumptions" (Lambert, 1995, p. 40).

Idea: Leadership Roles for Group Work

Nominated by their peers, students could take responsibility for different aspects of the group process. For instance, they could take on roles such as these:

Environmentalist: Makes sure everyone has a seat and furniture is arranged in an inclusive and focused way.

Facilitator: Works to ensure equitable participation.

Monitor: Monitors group work to ensure that the conversations are directed to the current task of the day.

Summarizer: Reports back to the class (or teacher) the group's progress and challenges.

Timekeeper: Keeps track of the time.

The Power of Student Reflections

Along with observing the group process in action, I also wanted to understand the individual perspective with this experience. Each time the classroom senate met, students wrote reflections about their experiences. Generally, they were open-ended in design, meaning that it was up to the student to decide what was significant about that day's legislative work. These reflections provided me with another layer of understanding the events that were emerging within our senate experience.

Reflections From the First Republican Caucus

These student reflections confirmed my impressions of what I had noticed in their first party caucus.

❏ I was not happy with how our Republican Party caucus went. I thought that people were not taking it seriously enough and we didn't get much done. (Amanda)

❏ The Republican Party . . . started out okay but then went downhill. No one was paying attention to anyone else. It was a nightmare. (Abigail)

Written reflections provide a channel for students to take account of the day's activity and their participation within it. Then too, these candid reflections serve as feedback loops to the teacher. What appears to be working in the curriculum drama? What issues need to be addressed? What should be the next steps?

Teacher as Political Consultant

When the Republicans met again, I decided to approach them as a "political consultant." My intent was to convey their unique position of power within the classroom senate. At the time of this experience, the Republicans held a slim majority in the U.S. Senate.

Upon receiving permission from Republican senators to speak at their caucus, I removed my "observer" tag and replaced it with "political consultant." I sat with them as they gathered together. Once everyone was seated, I introduced myself as a consultant from the Republican National Party.

Constructed Senate: Teacher as Political Consultant

After introducing myself to the Republican group as a political consultant, I said the following to them:

Currently, Republicans are in the majority in the U.S. Senate. That means that most people in this country who voted decided to elect Republican senators—not senators from the other party. So as the political group in this senate, you are also in the majority. This means you are responsible for representing the popular will of the voters. You can act upon this power and push a political agenda that reflects this strength. Or you can give the advantage to the Democrats. The choice is yours. Any questions? (*There were none.*)

After my "consultation," I promptly left the group, removed my "political consultant" tag, and replaced it with the "observer" tag. I sat a distance from them and watched them at work. The group began to identify key issues that they were concerned about, and they decided to split into committees to discuss these topics in more detail. Each committee was then charged with the task of drafting a statement about this issue. I soon left the room, as I wanted to see how the Democrats were doing.

Constantly Monitoring the Experience

Curriculum drama demands constant vigilance and mindfulness. As can be seen from the beginning phase of this experience, I took notice of what was happening within emerging situations. I listened to student conversations. What was being said and what was not being said? When and why did students break from the senate? Was it confusion? Resistance? Adolescent humor? What were different ways that people reacted to this situation? How could I help students step back into the legislative world of the classroom senate?

As you may remember, at this point the classroom senate had two separate groups. How did I monitor both groups? As I could not be everywhere at once, I was on the move constantly. Depending upon the circumstances, there were days when I spent more time observing one group than the other. Student reflections helped to fill in the gaps and kept me informed with the range of individual experiences that students had within the senate.

Another way that I kept up with events emerging from this classroom experience was by taking time to have informal side conversations with individual students. These take but a minute, and yet they provide such helpful information. Interestingly, these conversations provide a further shift in the classroom power dynamic. It is the students situated within the classroom senate who know the story. Whether they are at the center of activity or on the periphery of it, they have a perspective that I might not have from simply observing them. For this reason, I engaged students in occasional side conversations to find out the latest update from the classroom senate.

**Constructed Senate: A Side Conversation
With a Republican Senator**

Concerned about the Republican group, I had a side conversation with one of their members after their second meeting as a party.

Catherine: How are things going with the Republicans?

Chris: I think we really pulled together and started to think as one.

Catherine: What enabled you to start thinking as one?

Chris: Well, I think we opened our minds up a little bit and expanded it. We thought about what the party meant to us. . . . It took time to think about it.

Students needed time to grapple with ideas and to "think outside of their own worlds and ponder alternative possibilities" (Wolf, 1995, p. 133). After their first party caucus, the Republican group began to show a collaborative sense of acceptance, direction, and investment in their work. They were not mocking their political party or making disparaging remarks about the senate experience. As Chris put it, "We started to think as one."

Summary

This chapter explored the steps to build a political context within the classroom senate. Students first explored the meaning of "Republican" and "Democrat" through a series of research tasks. Upon being assigned to a particular party within the classroom senate, students then collaborated to construct their own political agenda.

This chapter emphasized the importance of building belief in a new classroom world. Sometimes, however, the unexpected dilemma occurred. Drawing from classroom experience, I provided ideas for working through these situations.

What's Next?

The next chapter, "Holding an Election: Engaging in Multiple Entry Points" examines how curriculum drama creates situations where students develop initiative and participate in unique ways within the transformed world of the classroom senate. Students engage in a high stakes senate election, and this galvanizes them to grapple with issues of political strategy, party loyalty, and the unpredictable nature of a secret ballot election.

5

Holding an Election

Engaging in Multiple Entry Points

Curriculum drama has many permutations. For example, some years in the classroom senate, the students and I decide to focus our energies on legislative activity; other years we decide to construct its political landscape before we engage in the activity of lawmaking.

This chapter and the one preceding it are focused on developing the political world within the classroom senate. Depending upon goals and available time frame, you may decide to skim this chapter and the previous one for background purposes only and then proceed to Chapter 6, which describes how students engage in the activity of making legislation.

In the activities in this chapter, students examine the nature of political strategy within the classroom senate. Emerging events propel students to take initiative, devise strategy, and engage in a high-stakes senate election. Table 5.1 outlines the key work within this phase of the experience.

The final segment of this chapter "Curriculum Drama in Action: President Pro Tempore Election" describes the sequence of events that took place within our constructed senate.

Setting the Stage

The teaching of content often happens when questions and issues emerge from the students' senate experience. Over the course of a few sessions, the class has been purposely divided and working in two separate groups—one called "Democrats," the other "Republicans."

Table 5.1   Plan of Action: Developing Leadership, Engaging in Strategy

Topics	Situation	Session
Setting the Stage	Class meeting	1
Electing Leaders Within the Party	Party caucus	1
Consulting With a Blueprint— President Pro Tempore	Class meeting	1
Thinking Strategically	Party caucus	1
Secret Ballot Election	Event	1

Bring the entire class together for a meeting. Pose open-ended questions to trigger student reflections.

- How would you describe your group's experience in constructing a political agenda?
- What challenges are you encountering with the group process?

Classroom Practice:
Holding an Election

There are many times when the class has an opportunity to run an election. Use this as a springboard for teaching social studies. This chapter provides ideas for holding an election that triggers student engagement and imagination.

As the teacher, you may have formed your own impressions as you have taken time to observe the proceedings in both groups. Nonetheless, this provides an opportunity for students to make public the work and challenges that they are facing. In this way, they will be informed about what is occurring across the political aisle.

Constructed Senate: Reflecting Upon the Process

As Democrats and Republicans, the students had been working in separate groups. By holding a class meeting and bringing the two groups together, issues emerged that helped to determine our next steps in the classroom senate.

Mary: Well, I was in the Democrat group. It was a bit confusing at first. But soon we got organized. We agreed upon a system where one of us had the job of calling on people who had their hands raised.

> **Jorge:** Well, I was in the Republican group. We didn't spend time to get organized. It was hell. No one seemed to be listening. I left with a huge headache!

Class meetings provide an opportunity for individuals to reflect upon their group work, to learn how their experience compares with that of others, and to set the stage for the next experience. As can be seen in the dialogue above, leadership was identified as an issue with the Republicans. Given their families' political backgrounds, it was not surprising that the Republicans had initial difficulty getting started (see Chapter 4 for more details). As a result of this discussion, students wanted to know who is in charge of a political party and how this leadership is determined.

Student questions, grapplings, and issues, based on their own experience within the classroom senate, provide the grist for learning new content. I took this opportunity to introduce them to the terms *party leader* and *party whip*.

Political Terminology: Party Leader and Whip

Party Leader: This person guides the party's legislative initiatives through Congress. These individuals are also called the majority leader (leading the majority party) and minority leader (leading the minority party).

Party Whip: This person assists the party leader and motivates members to vote for legislation that is backed by the party.

SOURCE: Virtual Reference Desk at http://www.senate.gov

Would students be interested in adopting these leadership positions within their classroom senate? If so, what will be the process for determining who gets which position?

Electing Leaders Within the Party

Effective leadership depends upon the collaboration of one's peers. In your class, discuss with students the qualifications for a strong leader (e.g., unifier of ideas, strong listener) and for someone who makes a strong party whip (e.g., strategic thinker, motivator). Urge students to cast a wide net for viable candidates and to move beyond those who are usually elected to leadership positions.

An Idea: Extending Leadership Positions

Rather than having one person for party leader and one for party whip, students could devise leadership in other ways. Here are two other options:

Shared Leadership: Two people are co–party leaders; two people are co-whips.

Team Leadership: Multiple positions create the leadership team (e.g., party leader, chief assistant to the party leader, deputy assistant to the party leader).

Each political group needs to spend time deciding upon their leadership structure and how they plan to elect their leaders.

Slowing Down the Process to Determine Leadership

Rather than determine leadership right away in their political groups, have students wait a few sessions until they become comfortable with their designated group. This provides time for leadership to naturally emerge.

Political Terminology: Majority and Minority Parties

There are continual shifts in which political party belongs to the majority or the minority. It depends upon which political party has more members in either house of Congress.

U.S. Senate Majority Party: This is the party that holds the most members in the U.S. Senate.

U.S. Senate Minority Party: This is the party that does not hold the majority in the U.S. Senate.

Are there students who want to break away from their political group? Create a twist in your senate, and propose the creation of an independent party.

Consulting With a Blueprint—President Pro Tempore

Upon electing party leaders and whips in the classroom senate and noting who has these positions in the U.S. Senate (http://www.senate.gov), ask the class if they know who is responsible for leading the senate. Where can they go to find out the answer?

Have students take note of the U.S. Constitution:

The Vice President of the United States shall be President of the Senate, but shall have no Vote, unless they be equally divided. (U.S. Constitution, Article 1, section 3, clause 4)

The Senate shall choose their other officers, and also a president pro tempore, in the absence of the Vice President or when he shall exercise the office of President of the United States. (U.S. Constitution, Article 1, section 3, clause 5)

In current times, the role of president pro tempore is largely ceremonial. It is the majority leader who facilitates, not necessarily leads, the business of the senate (Barone & Cohen, 2003).

Classroom Senate: Power of President Pro Tempore

Unlike the tradition in the U.S. Senate, where the president pro tempore is a long-standing member of the majority party, the practice in the classroom senate can be to create an alternative. Have both parties nominate a candidate for this position. In a subsequent election, the senators can elect by secret ballot one of these two individuals to lead the classroom senate.

The teacher may be tempted to take on the role of vice president and lead the classroom senate. But why? It is the student, not the teacher, who needs the opportunity and practice of leadership. Let the students have the opportunity to run their senate.

Political Terminology: President Pro Tempore

President Pro Tempore: This person serves as the temporary leader of the U.S. Senate, when the vice president of the United States is absent. By custom, this position is given to the longest-serving member of the majority party.

Duties: This person decides points of order and enforces decorum within the U.S. Senate chamber.

Change of Command: The president pro tempore is third in line to succeed the president (after the vice president and speaker of the house).

SOURCE: Byrd (1995).

Before each group determines its candidate for president pro tempore, draw connections between how the classroom senate works and how the U.S. Senate works. Table 5.2 compares these contexts.

Table 5.2   Points of Comparison: Leadership Positions

	Classroom Senate	*U.S. Senate*
Whip	2	2
Party Leader	2	2
President Pro Tempore	1	1
Vice President	0	1

Once students have determined their respective candidates for president pro tempore and have begun discussion on election strategy, expose the challenge that the minority party faces in this event. The following dialogue triggered a great deal of tension in my classroom, but at the same time it brought to the surface a key question. How could members of the minority party possibly compete against the majority party?

Constructed Senate: Sharing a Hunch—Inciting Tension

I baited the students about the anticipated outcome of this election.

Catherine:	It seems clear to me who will win the president pro tempore election. Based on numbers alone, there are 13 Republicans and 12 Democrats in our classroom senate (*pause*). But do people always vote for their party?
Jill: **(Democrat)**	Well, for me it is frankly not clear. I feel that a good leader is most important. I'm not planning on paying attention to which party the candidates are from. A good leader will represent the entire senate, not just one party.
Abigail: **(Republican)**	That's right. I don't think it's fair to choose until we see and hear the speeches from both candidates.
Sue: **(Democrat)**	I'd like to ask my colleagues in the Republican Party a direct question. Should you vote for who will truly support your beliefs or who you think you **should** (*spoken emphasis*) vote for?
Leah: **(Republican)**	I don't know. Don't Republicans vote Republican and Democrats vote Democrat?
Sue: **(Democrat)**	But are you **really** (*spoken emphasis*) a Republican?

As can be seen above, students participated in this discussion, not from a distanced study of the political process, but rather from their own, up-close situated experience (Greeno, 1991; Lave & Wenger, 1991) within the classroom senate. By candidly sharing their views about the election, students became more aware of the varied ways that peers were approaching this experience. Voting for president pro tempore became a complex and messy issue.

This also underscores the importance of holding class meetings throughout the course of a curriculum drama. These sessions help to create a spirit of collective inquiry and social connection. This is particularly important when the class is divided into separate groups (e.g., Republicans/Democrats) and when they are confronting different situations (e.g., the power differential between the majority and minority parties).

On another note, curriculum drama challenges the teacher to interact as a curious observer and active listener. For instance, when the classroom senate is in motion and students step into their constructed positions, I work to identify political tension points, hidden agendas, and potential conflicts. When the class steps out of their constructed positions and gathers to discuss their legislative experience, I can use my neutral position to bring emerging dissonance to their attention and scrutiny. I am careful, however, not to reveal political strategies or individual trusts.

Extension

The election for president pro tempore creates an ideal context for discussing relevant issues in a democracy (e.g., fair elections).

❑ In our democracy, when is there transparency (e.g., public record), and when is there protection of privacy (e.g., citizen casting a vote)?

❑ In our election for president pro tempore, what is more fair—holding a public vote or casting secret ballots?

Thinking Strategically

Meet separately with the elected leader and whip from each party. Discuss with them their preliminary ideas for getting their candidates elected. How unified are the members of the majority party in supporting their candidate? How will the minority party attempt to obtain crossover votes?

An Idea: Splitting the Ticket—Political Strategy for the Minority Party

Along with nominating a candidate from their own party for president pro tempore, the minority party could also nominate a second candidate from the majority party. This other candidate could split the majority hold by drawing votes away from their primary candidate.

The classroom senate does not follow a preset, rigid procedure. Instead, it is open to constant adaptation and creations. Splitting the ticket might be teacher initiated or student initiated.

The following dialogue occurred within the minority party in my classroom. They began to explore the idea of obtaining a crossover vote from a member of the majority party. Through this discussion, political affiliation began to be viewed in dynamic ways. Under the right circumstances, the Democrats could envision how party loyalty could change within the Republican Party.

Constructed Senate: Thinking Strategically

The Democrats discussed their position as members of the minority party in the upcoming senate election.

Mike: All that matters is getting our candidate elected to be president pro tempore. **We** (*bolded for spoken emphasis*) want a Democrat to be elected.

Tom: Unless all the Republicans vote for their people and then. . . .

Mary: How many **more** (*spoken emphasis*) Republicans are there?

Mike: They have 13, we have 12. Obviously we are **all** (*spoken emphasis*) going to vote Democrat. (*Everyone nods in assent.*)

Jesse: There must be **one** (*spoken emphasis*) Republican that we could sway to vote Democrat.

As can be seen in the above dialogue, there were swirls of ideas happening within this student-run meeting. On one hand, Mike, the elected party leader, emphasized the importance of staying loyal to the party and "getting our candidate elected." On the other hand, Jesse noted the tentative nature of political membership and how "there must be one Republican" who could vote on their side.

Student Reflections

For homework the night before, or in the beginning session of class on the day of the election, have students write out their positions—who they plan to vote for and why. This helps students think through their actions ahead of time. It also provides you with an idea of which students have already determined their choice for president pro tempore and which are waiting to hear the speeches before making a decision.

While the majority of students planned to vote for their respective party's candidate, the nature of secret ballot elections created a situation where students could use the cloak of privacy to make their final decision.

Constructed Senate: Thinking About the Upcoming Election

Rather than follow party line, one student expressed a more independent view.

Jill: (Democrat)	I am going in with an open mind. I will listen and make a choice based on whether or not I feel that person is going to do the best job. I may vote Democrat, and I may vote Republican. A good president pro tempore will look at the bills that will benefit our nation, not just his or her party.

Secret Ballot Election: An Event

Work with both parties to schedule a date for the president pro tempore election. Here are suggested ways to set the stage for this defining event.

Tools of the Trade

Desk cards serve to remind students that for this event they are now publicly positioned as elected officials, and they need to refer to one another with the honorific title "Senator." Desk cards identify each senator's political party and state. If a senator is elected to a leadership position, the card includes this information as well.

Desk cards are simple to make. Fold a large index card in half with the blank side facing out. On the blank side, print the student's information so that it is visible to all (e.g., in 40-point type). For example, Michael Blitz, the Republican senator from Michigan, who was also the party leader, had the card shown here.

Ballots prepared ahead of time can help to create an orderly process. Make sure there is one ballot for each senator present.

Sen. Michael Blitz

Michigan

Party Leader

> **Constructed Senate: Agenda for President Pro Tempore Election**
>
> Students and I constructed the agenda for defining moments in the classroom senate.
>
> Speeches
>
> Secret ballot election
>
> Election result

Setting the Stage

Arrange desks so that the Republicans are on one side of the room and the Democrats are on the other. Place desk cards at these locations where each senator is to sit.

Post an agenda in public view to indicate the sequence of events that will take place within this session.

Curriculum drama is dynamic and unpredictable. The following section explores the course of events that happened when students in my class engaged in the secret ballot election for president pro tempore.

Curriculum Drama in Action: President Pro Tempore Election

On the morning of the election, the two parties held caucuses to review their candidates' speeches for president pro tempore. I went from one group to the other to observe their work.

Republicans

Alex, the Republican candidate, practiced his speech before his party and listened to peer feedback. Students working as peer coaches directed Alex to fine tune parts of his speech.

Both Eli and Amanda took it upon themselves to provide Alex with timely advice.

Constructed Senate: Rehearsing a Speech

Alex, as the Republican candidate for president pro tempore, rehearsed his speech. His team of speech coaches provided feedback.

Amanda: I think the speech is really, really good, but you have to be careful not to laugh in some parts.

Eli: And don't say "neuter" instead of "nurture."

Alex: *(nods head in acknowledgment and smiles)*

Amanda: In the part where it says, "I have a vision for a bright future," don't laugh at that. If you take it seriously, they'll take it seriously. I mean if you laugh at your own speech, they will laugh at it.

Democrats

Pat, the Democratic candidate, had been sick for a few days before the election. She arrived back at school on the day of the election. She had completely forgotten about this event. The party feverishly crafted a speech in the minutes before the election.

Setting the Stage

Before the actual election, the senate engaged in a sequence of activities to build belief in this defining event.

Interacting in a Different Way to the Environment

When students bounded into the classroom, they soon stopped short. Each desk had a desk card with the honorific title "Senator" followed by the student's full name. This marked a break from the ordinary, as we had never used desk cards.

In addition, seats were assigned and grouped by political affiliations. The Republicans and Democrats sat in separate locations around a circle of desks. This helped to make the familiar seem unfamiliar; typically students sat where they wished in the classroom. Figure 5.1 shows this classroom arrangement.

Figure 5.1   Senate Election: Classroom Arrangement

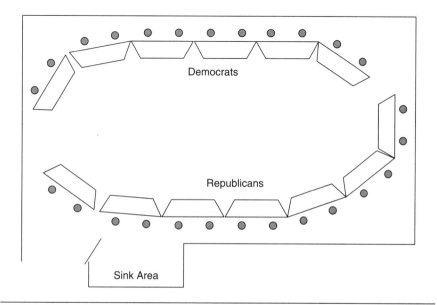

Participating in a Quorum Call

Once all were seated, I announced that there needed to be a *quorum* before our legislative body could proceed with plans for the election. This brought increased attention to the upcoming event and it seemed to make it more "official."

Constructed Senate: Quorum Call

Jorge as Senator Santos, the majority leader, conducted the administrative task of calling a quorum before the senate began the election proceedings. With gavel in hand, he tapped the desk and began speaking.

Sen. Santos: (Jorge)	Today is March 3rd and I bring this senate to order (*taps gavel again*). Before the senate conducts an election for our president pro tempore, we need to make sure that we have a quorum. When I call your name, say "here." Senator Belt?
Sen. Belt: (Bill)	Here.
Sen. Santos: (Jorge)	Senator Blitz?
Sen. Blitz: (Mike)	Here

Political Terminology: Quorum and Quorum Call

Quorum: A majority of the members in a legislative body

Quorum call: A procedure used to determine if there is a sufficient number of legislative members present to conduct business.

SOURCE: Virtual Reference Desk at http://www.senate.gov

Speeches

After the quorum call, each party formally announced their elected leaders (e.g., party leader and whip) and their candidate for president pro tempore.

Extensions

Time permitting, students could prepare speeches in support of their candidates for president pro tempore. To prepare for this task, students could explore ideas and rhetoric from memorable political speeches in the past. If your school has a speech department, perhaps they can support this endeavor.

Alex, the Republican candidate, volunteered to give his speech first. He stood in front of the class and faced the senators. Holding the two page typed speech in front of him, he spoke clearly and seriously. His delivery was calm and poised. Toward the end of the speech, he was skillfully placing emphasis on key words and phases.

Constructed Senate: From the Speech of the Republican Candidate

Alex, the Republican candidate for president pro tempore, delivered the following speech:

I have a vision (*pause*)

of a bright future for America.

A future (*voice becoming stronger*)

in which our economy **thrives** (*bolded for emphasis*)

and our people are educated and capable of making the right decisions for themselves.

A future in which **all** (*bolded for emphasis*)

children are nurtured and given a **fair** (*prolonged emphasis*) chance to succeed.

I will work my hardest to make this dream a reality (*sustained pause*) for our nation.

Students appeared riveted by this experience. Amanda, his informal speech coach, and Abigail, the main speechwriter, gripped one another's arm as Alex began his speech. When he finished, they spontaneously stood up and applauded.

Pat, the Democratic candidate, followed next. She got out of her chair and walked slowly to the front. She began speaking in a hoarse and somewhat shaky voice.

**Constructed Senate: From the
Speech of the Democratic Candidate**

Pat, the Democratic candidate for president pro tempore, emphasized the difference in character between herself and the opposing candidate. An excerpt follows:

> I will take responsibility for my actions thoroughly, unlike our other candidate. All of us know the Republican candidate and we know how much he strives to have power over others. With all due respect to the other candidate, look at him; then look at me. Seriously (*sustained pause*), who do you think would do the better job?

Pat and her colleagues gambled that this mud-slinging ploy would cause an immediate reaction from Alex, the Republican candidate. The room seemed to hold its breath in expectation of Alex's reaction. Interestingly, this speech came as a surprise, particularly as Pat was actually good friends with Alex. They were part of a tight peer group within the classroom.

Unexpectedly, Alex remained calm and did not react to Pat's provocation.

Learning From Experience: Reviewing Candidates' Speeches

In light of what occurred in this classroom situation, I took time in subsequent years to meet with the respective candidates to make sure that their speeches were well prepared and appropriate in tone.

Casting Ballots

After the speeches, I handed a ballot to each senator. In the moments before the ballots were collected, the whips from both parties stood up and walked around the room. They spoke quietly to some senators hoping to influence those who seemed undecided.

The class had requested that as clerk I should be the one to count the ballots. That day there were 24 students; one student (a member of the Republican Party) was absent. This meant that the senate had an equal number from both parties. Would people vote party line? If so, would there be a tie vote?

Election Result

After counting the ballots, I realized there was a clear winner. Sen. Alex Koch, the Republican candidate, had won 13 to 11. A Democrat had crossed over and voted Republican.

Who had voted for the other party? As it was a secret ballot election, there were parts to this story that were known to some, but not all. The identity of the Democrat who had crossed over to the Republican side remained a mystery.

Classroom Dilemma: Breaking Too Soon From an Event

Students applauded upon learning the results of the election. Spontaneously, many got out of their seats and moved around the classroom. They stood around chatting with their friends, and the conversation began to get loud. Before long, I became aware that not all their conversations were related to the senate experience. It had become a mere social event.

Creating a Media Event

Wanting to return to the drama of the election, I decided to hold a roving press conference. In this way, I hoped to create a situation where students could be pulled back to the senate reality. I decided to conduct on-the-spot interviews with senators. Fortunately, I had a video camera accessible. One of my students, Lee, eagerly agreed to be my camera person.

This was a good role for Lee. In the classroom setting, he was typically marginalized; he had difficulty reading social cues and was often teased by his peers. Behind the camera's eye, however, Lee seemed secure in his interactions with his classmates. In fact, as his classmates stood in position waiting to be interviewed, Lee gave them camera advice (e.g., stand closer together). They listened to him and followed his helpful recommendations.

With a press pass hanging from a string around my neck, I asked senators about their reaction to the election.

Constructed Senate: Press Coverage of Senate Election

Quiet and introspective, Senator Abigail Law was the main speechwriter for the Republican Party. She had unexpectedly found herself in the center of media activity and peer attention; her colleagues had been congratulating her on the speech she had crafted for Senator Koch.

Sen. Law: **(Abigail)**	I'm really pleased that the speech worked out. It worked out better than I thought it would. . . . I'm very pleased with how it sounded and how Alex read it.

When interviewed, Senator Alex Koch, the newly elected president pro tempore, acknowledged the work of his talented colleagues.

Sen. Koch: **(Alex)**	I am very happy that I won. I think that one of the main reasons is because I had such a good speechwriting team. A lot of credit has to go to my colleagues in the Republican Party . . . particularly Senator Law, the main speechwriter.

Summary

This chapter explored the multiple entry points for building belief in the curriculum drama. In their respective political groups, the students decided upon their leaders (e.g., party leader, party whip, candidate for president pro tempore), engaged in political strategy, and grappled with the decision of who to vote for in a high-stakes senate election. In addition, the generative nature of this approach created unique opportunities. Situations emerged where students used their own talents (e.g., as speechwriter) to support their leader's candidacy.

What's Next?

In the next chapter I describe activities in which students engage in the practice of writing legislation and working in committee. This creates another entry point within the classroom senate. Along with being members of a political group, students become affiliated with a particular bill that they wrote and a committee where they review a number of different legislative ideas.

6

Current Events

Doing Legislative Work

Curriculum drama builds upon the interests, energies, and initiatives of the classroom participants as a way for students to connect in substantive ways to the intended content material. The previous chapter explored how multiple entry points helped to develop a sense of belief in the ongoing activities emerging within the classroom senate.

This chapter explores interactions *within* a community of practice, as students face the challenge of proposing legislation based on their personal life experiences and understandings. Spurred by "real topics contemplated in everyday life" (Kuhn, 1986, p. 501), students become absorbed in their positions and responsibilities within this legislative experience. Table 6.1 outlines the situations that emerge during this phase of the curriculum drama.

The final segment of this chapter, "Curriculum Drama in Action: Committee Work," describes the inner workings and challenges of students as they engage in the process of working in committee.

Classroom Practice: Engaging in Current Events

Rather than holding classroom discussions or having students write reports on current events, challenge students to construct legislation that addresses a contemporary issue. This chapter provides ideas for students to engage in and interact with national issues.

Table 6.1   Plan of Action: Developing Ideas for Legislation

Topic	Situation	Sessions

Setting the Stage
    Powers of Congress
    Coming up with a legislative idea
	Class meetings	2–3

Consulting With a Blueprint and Constructing Legislation	Class meeting/ Homework	1
Introducing Legislation	Event	1
Appraising Legislation	Party caucus	1
Engaging in Committee Work	Committee sessions	3

Setting the Stage

Begin by finding out what students' law-related experiences and understandings have been. Have they encountered

- federal laws (e.g., seat belt law, minimum wage, voting eligibility)?
- state laws (e.g., state highway speed limits, legal drinking age, legal driving age)?
- city or town laws (e.g., local traffic ordinances, parking rules, town curfew)?

Powers of Congress

As a class, read section 8 of the U.S. Constitution. Explore the delegated powers of Congress and how they relate to the legislator's role of making laws. Draw attention to the final clause:

Extensions

❑ Hold a class, small group, or panel discussion on the characteristics of a good law.

❑ Take a field trip around the school's neighborhood. Have students conduct a survey of the legal-based signs around them.

To make all laws which shall be necessary and proper for carrying into execution the foregoing powers, and all other powers vested by this constitution in the government of the United States, or in any department or officer thereof. (U.S. Constitution, Article 1, section 8, clause 18)

Known as the *elastic clause,* this clause gives Congress the power to make all "necessary and proper" laws for the federal government.

This extends the powers specifically delegated to Congress in Article 1, section 8, clauses 1–17.

Using selected readings from a civics textbook, review the step-by-step process of the legislative system and how it involves the two houses of Congress (U.S. House of

> **Political Terminology: Elastic Clause**
>
> *Elastic Clause:* Congress makes all "necessary and proper" laws for the federal government. This clause is located in the U.S. Constitution, Article I, section 8.

Representatives and U.S. Senate). Examine also how the executive branch executes the laws and how the judicial branch makes subsequent rulings on whether a contested law is aligned to the U.S. Constitution.

Table 6.2 compares the process of passing laws in the classroom senate with that of the U.S. Congress.

Table 6.2   Points of Comparison: From Legislation to Law

	Classroom Senate	*U.S. Congress*
Legislation Approved by the Senate	Yes	Yes*
Legislation Approved by the House	Not applicable	Yes*
Legislation Signed Into Law by the President	Not applicable	Yes (unless overturned by two-thirds of Congress)
*Legislation may originate in either the Senate or the House.		

> **An Idea: Creating a Congress Within the School**
>
> Consider extending the reach of this senate experience and getting your colleagues involved with it. Could another class transform to a classroom house of representatives so as to vote on a classroom senate bill?

Coming Up With a Legislative Idea

Invite students to use their life experiences and perceptions of the world around them to review the legislative activities they have done so far in their classroom senate. This work might trigger ideas for constructing their own legislation:

Political Agenda

Encourage students to consider the political agenda that they constructed within their party caucus (see Chapter 4). Could they create legislation based on an idea from their party's platform?

State Research

Remind students to consider issues that surfaced in their state research (see Chapter 3). Could they construct legislation based on a state issue that has national interest?

Extensions: Preparing the Class for Lawmaking

To extend this unit on constructing legislation, students could engage in the following activities:

Survey: Have students ask adults about federal laws that they would like to repeal, change, or initiate.

Art: Have students construct a collage from magazine or newspaper pictures showing societal or economic inequities. These images could then become the trigger for discussing ideas for bills that would address contemporary issues (e.g., homelessness, firearms).

Guest Speaker: Invite a state senator or representative to talk about bills that she or he is working on at the state level. Or invite a representative from a major advocacy group (e.g., Children's Defense Fund) to talk about issues that the organization is promoting at the national level.

Existing Legislation

Students might want to explore http://www.senate.gov to locate legislation that is being considered in the U.S. Senate. Could they modify previously constructed legislation from the U.S. Senate?

Previous Legislation

If you construct this experience each year, locate bills that were developed from the previous classroom senate. Could students adapt a constructed bill from last year's classroom senate?

An Idea: Devising Legislation Through Student Interests

Bridge the task of devising legislation to topics that are directly relevant to students' lives.

Student Interest	Societal Concern	Legislative Topic
Art	After school time	Fully funded and supervised youth centers devoted to the advancement of the arts (drama, dance, music and visual arts)
Driving	Car passenger safety	Drivers over 75 years of age must take yearly vision and reflex tests
Fashion	Sweat shops	Regulate labor practices in the clothing industry
Food	Nutrition	Mandate the practice of serving only healthy foods in public schools
Sports	Health	Institute gym or exercise classes in public schools

---

Consulting With a Blueprint and Constructing Legislation

Before students take on the challenge of constructing their own piece of legislation, have them explore the structure of a bill. Have them go to http://www.senate.gov (click to Active Legislation) and examine three pieces of U.S. Senate legislation. What common structures do they notice in these bills? Working with students, develop a format for constructing a classroom bill.

For homework or in a class session, have each student individually construct a bill. Reassure the class that their bills are in a preliminary phase of construction. Through the process of peer feedback in committee, witness testimony in legislative hearings, and teacher feedback, legislative ideas will become more detailed and developed.

Shortcut

Resource G contains a format for creating a bill. Students might want to compare its structure to that of its counterparts in the U.S. Senate.

Introducing Legislation: An Event

Once each senator has constructed an individual bill, mark the moment by organizing an official legislative session. Have senators read their bills before their colleagues. Log in each bill and give it an official senate number (e.g., S 121).

Setting the Stage

Schedule a date for a formal senate session. An elected senate leader (e.g., president pro tempore, party leader) could run this session. Use tools of the trade to set the stage for this ceremonial event:

> *Desk cards* on everyone's desks remind students that they are now publicly positioned as senators, and they need to use the language of the senate.

> *Use a gavel* to alert senators that the business of the senate is about to begin. Only the designated leader may use this instrument (or any tool that could serve this purpose).

> *Use a hopper.* A hopper is a box where bills are placed for future consideration by a legislative body. Locate a cardboard box and attach a sign with the word "hopper" on it. After each bill is given a senate number, place this legislation in the hopper.

Shortcut

Rather than stage an event, post each student's bill in a prominent location in the classroom. Provide post-its to each member of the class. Upon reading someone's bill, a classmate could then write a constructive comment or suggestion and post it next to the legislation. After everyone has reviewed the class's legislation and directed comments toward some bills, remove the post-its and give this written peer feedback and your own comments to each lawmaker.

Constructed Senate: Introducing Senate Legislation

Standing up and tapping the wooden gavel twice on his desk, Sen. Alex Koch, the elected president pro tempore, quickly got his colleagues' attention.

Sen. Koch: (Alex)	Welcome, senators. I call the senate to order (*taps gavel again on wooden table*). Today is Wednesday, March 6th. The senate is now in session (*taps gavel a final time*).

	For today, we will formally introduce our legislation to the senate. At a later time, we will respond to these ideas and debate them. For now we are simply listening to the ideas in each senator's bill. Any questions? Senator Brown?
Sen. Brown: (Ellen)	Wait a minute! Can we still change the bill?
Sen. Koch: (Alex)	(*conferring with me*) Yes. Until it is signed into law, legislation is simply a draft. It can be completely changed until then. Okay then. The first bill is entitled "Clean Air." Senator Mill, I believe this is your bill.
Sen. Mill: (Mary)	(*reading from bill*) The bill's title is "Clean Air." Its purpose is to help keep the air clean from factories' smoke and smog. Provision: We would like to have 60 percent of all factories in the United States to have filtering screens (*passes bill back to Sen. Koch*).
Sen. Koch: (Alex)	I dub this bill "S 125" (*places bill inside a cardboard box with the term "hopper" written prominently on all sides*).

As may be noted from this dialogue, students listened first to Alex announce the title of the bill, and then they heard its author publicly read its complete text. This enabled students to hear the full range of legislation being proposed within their senate.

Along with the introduction of the hopper and the gavel, students'

> **Political Terminology**
>
> *Hopper:* This is a box where proposals for laws are placed for consideration by a legislative body.
>
> ---
>
> SOURCE: *Oxford American Dictionary* (1980).

language helped to define this senate experience. In his first session as president pro tempore, Senator Koch decided on his own accord to spice his language with such terms as "order of business" and "dub." In addition, when a classmate asked a question, he referred to her as "Senator Brown," not as "Ellen." Then again, Ellen as Senator Brown posed a question about legislative procedure not to the teacher, but rather to the president pro tempore. This session in the classroom senate included the use of new objects, new terminology, and new ways of interacting with classmates.

Appraising Legislation

Once all bills have been given a senate number, have the party leaders meet with members from their own respective parties. In this session, individual bills can be discussed, questioned, and revised before they go to committee.

Constructed Senate: Appraising a Bill in the Democratic Caucus

Students shared their legislative ideas with one another. In this instance, Mary reads aloud her clean air bill and faces a question from a classmate.

Mary: My bill is to keep the air clean from factories and smog. In the year 2010, 60 percent of all factories in the United States will have filtering screens over their chimneys, so that when the smog and smoke come up from the factories, it will be filtered. Any questions? Katie?

Katie: Do you know how much the filters cost?

Mary: I don't know.

Katie: Do you think it will be a big amount?

As can be seen above, the process of questioning uncovered further issues that needed to be researched with Mary's bill. Katie had genuine concerns about the subsequent impact of this bill; she worried that expensive environmental safeguards might lead to companies reducing their work force:

> We know about our economy and how we are in debt. . . .
> I mean some people have had their parents lose jobs, and we
> know how hard it is for them. We don't want people to lose
> their jobs. We are really thinking about this stuff. We are doing
> this from experience.

The task of listening to one another and discussing legislative ideas propelled students to think in new ways. Writing and revising a bill became a meaningful endeavor. Questions and suggestions that were posed at this session spurred some lawmakers to clarify their ideas and rewrite their bills. Table 6.3 lists the legislative titles that have emerged from both parties within the constructed senate in my classroom.

Being coconstructors of the senate, students in my classroom constructed legislation on issues that they identified as being important. In some years, the party leaders and whips influence the lawmakers within their parties to make bills more aligned to each party's political agenda. In other years, students construct bills independent of political allegiances.

In the end, addressing issues that "seem to be important" is ultimately what we are aiming for with this experience. We want our

Table 6.3   Constructed Senate: Republican and Democratic Legislation

Topic	Republican	Democrat
Economy	- Help businesses in low income, highly populated areas - Job training and living wage careers for high school drop outs - Help for corporations planning to locate to areas hit by natural disasters	
Education	- School choice - Funding for families with students achieving high test scores - Abstinence education - Merit pay for teachers	- HIV/AIDS curriculum for all students - Condom distribution in schools
Energy	- Funding for Arctic oil exploration	- Funding for research and development of alternative fuel systems
Environment	- Reduce smokestack pollution	- Clean air by mandating filters on smokestacks - Increase gas mileage in new vehicles (cars, trucks, buses) - Make city buses electric or hybrids
Family and Health	- Faith-based community centers to care for homeless - Random drug testing in government funded recreation centers for youth	- Legalization of gay marriage and child adoption - Universal health care - Ready access to family planning clinics
Immigration		- Open door policy for all immigrants
Security	- National identification card - Mandatory draft or community service for all 18-year-olds	- Education for the incarcerated - Reducing crime by increasing security in major cities

students to craft bills that begin to address issues that are relevant to them.

Sponsoring bills is a way for students to support and become familiar with the legislative initiatives being proposed within their senate.

Constructed Senate: Aligning Bills to a Political Agenda

Senator Jorge Santos, the majority leader of the Republican group, noted how his colleagues constructed legislation based on personal relevance rather than on political alignment:

> Well, in our group we are not really following the guidelines that we had set for ourselves earlier in the party platform. We are just addressing the issues that seem to be important.

Extension: Bill Sponsorship

As a way for students to interact with one another and connect with their legislative ideas, include a session where students could approach classmates and seek sponsorship of their bill. Inform students that sponsorship does not mean that an individual is under any obligation to favor the bill when it comes time for the senate to vote on it. A senator might sponsor a bill at one phase, but decide to oppose it at a later time.

Engaging in Committee Work

Have the party leaders from the classroom senate work together to group the individual bills into similar categories.

Shortcut

Rather than have student leaders engage in the task of placing bills in related committees, use your own authority to make these decisions. Then share your decision-making process with the class.

I recommend that each committee consider four to six bills. If some legislative categories do not have enough bills, combine two smaller committees into a larger one.

Table 6.4 uses the committee structure as a point of comparison between the classroom senate and the U.S. Senate. In the U.S. Senate,

---

Constructed Senate: Committees

There were five committees in our constructed senate:

- ☐ Economic Development and Energy
- ☐ Education
- ☐ Environmental Affairs
- ☐ Family and Health
- ☐ Security and Immigration

Table 6.4   Points of Comparison: Committee Structure

	Classroom Senate	*U.S. Senate*
Number of Bills	25	several thousand
Standing Committees	5–6	17
Committee Assignments	student or teacher decision	nominated by the political party

the legislators are assigned to a committee where they might not necessarily examine legislation that they initiated or cosponsored. This is a different practice from the one used in the classroom senate, where senators follow their legislation into committee. For instance, if a student's bill is centered on education, then that student will be assigned to the education committee.

Constructed Senate: Official Announcement of Committee Assignments

Committee assignments can be another opportunity to stage an official event within the classroom senate:

President pro tempore   (standing up and tapping gavel): Welcome, senators. I call the senate to order. Today I will announce your committee assignments. Before doing so, however, I would like to thank the two party leadersfor working on this task. They were the ones whodecided which committee you will be in.

The members in the Environment Affairs Committee are

- ❑ Republican Senator Brian Kalim

- ❑ Democrat Senator Mary Mill

- ❑ Democrat Senator Jesse Small

- ❑ Democrat Senator Tom Wright

Shortcut

Rather than staging an event where committees and their members are officially announced, post this information in a prominent location in the classroom.

Preliminary Tasks in Committee

Arrange time for students in their new committees to meet and share their legislation. What patterns do they notice about these bills? Which bills address national concerns? How could one bill incorporate ideas from another piece of legislation?

Electing a Committee Chairperson

Another task is to elect a committee chairperson. This individual is responsible for making sure the committee's work proceeds in an organized way. If the senate wants to be aligned to current partisan practice, each chairperson will be from the majority party.

Markup

This current phase of work is called a *markup*. Through the course of multiple work sessions, each committee develops the details of a piece of prioritized legislation. This might occur by combining comparable bills into a comprehensive piece of legislation, or it might occur by focusing on one piece of legislation and developing it further.

Students encounter new vocabulary and concepts in context; in this way new terms connect directly to their current activity within the senate.

Political Terminology: Markup

Markup: This is the process where proposed legislation is rewritten based on recommendations from congressional committees.

SOURCE: Virtual Reference Desk at http://www.senate.gov

"Touch Base" Meetings Before Committee Work

Each time there are scheduled committee meetings, bring the full class together first for a quick meeting. This helps to create a sense of coherence, focus, and direction within the experience. In these sessions, lasting no more than 5–10 minutes, focus on one particular topic that directly pertains to the work they are doing in committee. Here are some ideas:

- Review the intended goal of that day's committee work; Resource H shows a sample of committee tasks.
- Introduce ideas for how to develop provisions within legislation. Details could include such areas as ways to finance the bill,

incentives for individuals who are directly affected by this bill (e.g., tax cuts), and penalties for individuals who do not go along with this bill's provisions (e.g., fines).

- Share your own perspective on the patterns that you observed in the previous committee session. In general terms, what appears to be working? What appears to be a common challenge?

Extension: No Child Left Behind Act of 2001 (Public Law 107–110)

Explore a public law and its provisions. For instance, the No Child Left Behind Act of 2001 contains one provision where schools receive federal aid provided that upon request they give military recruiters . . . access to secondary school students' names, addresses, and telephone listings.

In another provision, schools that are unable to report adequate yearly progress on standardized test scores are subject to government scrutiny.

Research: Have students explore the public voting record of their U.S. senators to determine their positions on the No Child Left Behind Act.

Discuss: What has been the influence of No Child Left Behind in their own lives?

Activism: Have students write letters to their elected officials expressing their points of view on this law and providing recommendations on whether this law needs to be renewed, amended, or revoked.

As students are in the midst of appraising their classmates' legislation, they will be well positioned to critique U.S. Senate legislation.

Observing the Group Process in Committee

As an observer, spend time at each committee and then move on to another one. As you visit each group, select one or all of the following areas to observe:

- Inclusion: Are all members included in this group discussion?
- Focus: Is the current conversation centered on matters related to committee work?
- Activity: Does group work appear mindful, purposeful, and sustained?
- Order: Are committee members participating in an organized way?

Classroom Dilemma: Discord in Small Group Work

There will be times when a committee encounters a challenge that they can not handle. Perhaps it is related to the group process. Have some voices been excluded or has one voice dominated? Perhaps it is related to the nature of the task itself. Does the group understand their agenda?

Rather than approaching the situation from the standpoint of teacher as adult authority, consider these alternative roles:

- As a Concerned Colleague: Meet separately with the chairperson to discuss the situation and to brainstorm possible solutions.
- As an Invited Political Consultant: Meet with the entire committee to discuss the situation and to brainstorm possible solutions.
- As an Interim Cochairperson: Meet with the committee for a certain amount of time to model and instill an organized system of committee work.
- As a Coach: Meet with an individual student and provide guidance in how to best collaborate, negotiate, and compromise in a group setting.

Admittedly, it can be a daunting task to follow the simultaneous work of multiple student committees. How do you develop a sense of which group needs supervision and which group is working well independently? For those that appear to be challenged, how best can you guide them without taking over?

Unlike teacher directed lessons where the adult is in charge and makes key decisions, in curriculum drama the teacher and the students work together. Students have the freedom *and* responsibility to manage their own group process, while at the same time, the teacher actively takes steps to verify and assess their progress.

Idea: Keeping Track of Committee Work

Along with observing committees in action, here are three additional ideas for keeping up with committee developments:

Report Out: At the end of each committee session, have a spokesperson from each committee report to the class about its progress.

Write: To peer into the individual experience, have students write reflections about their time in committee. What decisions were made? What challenges were encountered?

Meet: Hold an informal session with just the committee chairpersons. Have each chairperson discuss the work and challenges within their committee.

Developing Legislation in Committee

Once all the committees have developed productive working relationships, have them review their respective bills. Committee members will then be well positioned to eventually construct prioritized legislation. These questions can help them in this process:

- How is this legislation relevant and timely?
- How does this legislation address national interests?
- To what extent is this legislation fair?

Observing Legislative Discussions in Committee

As an observer to these conversations, your focus now shifts from group process issues to the group's collective understandings about their committee's emerging legislation. These are questions to ask yourself, and possible tasks to follow up on, as you listen to their flow of ideas:

- What reference sources (e.g., Web sites, almanacs) could they access to develop deeper understandings about this legislative topic?
- What news articles have recently been published on this legislative topic?
- What organizations would support or oppose this legislative idea?

The process of creating legislation within committee can become an experience that deeply engages students with one another and with the world of legislation. Students draw upon the collective resourcefulness of their group to create viable legislation.

Constructed Senate: Committee Reflection

Tom, a member of the Environmental Committee, reflected upon the experience of constructing prioritized legislation with other committee members:

> It seems real because we have to do all this stuff that real senators have to do. I mean it is not that much fun to write bills. [Nonetheless] you can kind of use your own ideas and put down your ideas that you would do if you were a real senator.

While each committee needs to invest energy in its prioritized bill, committee members must also recognize that the senate may not have time to consider their legislation. For instance, in our constructed senate, the students and I only managed to fully address one, sometimes two, pieces of legislation each year.

Informing students in advance about the senate process helps to prepare them for emerging events. In this way, they can work with intensity in their committee but not get overly invested in their prioritized legislation.

Constructed Senate: Letters to Constituents

After each committee determined their prioritized legislation, senators wrote letters to their constituents:

Dear Fellow Americans,
   Here in Washington we are trying hard to come up with an easy, low-cost way to help the environment. As you already know, many major cities are having problems keeping their air pollution down. We have come up with a bill to address this problem. . . .
                              — (Mary, Committee on Environmental Affairs)

In letters to constituents, students have the opportunity to show how their committee's legislation is both relevant and timely.

Homework assignments (e.g., constructing legislation, letter to constituents) help students sustain belief in their constructed position within the curriculum drama. At the same time, these assignments approximate the practice (e.g., lawmaking) and the responsibility (e.g., keeping constituents informed) of elected office in Congress.

Word of Advice: Group Work

This portion of the classroom senate positions students in small group settings as committee members. How can we ensure that each group works at the same approximate pace as the others?

Meet Deadline: Set a deadline for when all committees will present their prioritized legislation. Ensure that each committee meets the deadline.

Trust the Process: Remind all that until the bill is voted on, committees can continue to mark it up.

Shortcut

Rather than having students construct their own bills and determine their committee's prioritized legislation, provide the class with a current law (e.g., No Child Left Behind). Have students review its stated goals and selected provisions. Engage the class in a discussion about this law. Does this fit their criteria for a good law? What changes would they propose to make it a better law?

Extension: Discussion—Should Citizens Obey Unjust Laws?

Explore with the class the historical context for such laws as

❏ Indian Removal Act of 1830
❏ Fugitive Slave Law of 1850

Curriculum Drama in Action: Committee Work

Within my classroom senate one year, there were four members in the Committee on Environmental Affairs, one Republican (Brian) and three Democrats (Jesse, Mary, and Tom). Together they negotiated with one another about including aspects of their own bills into one comprehensive piece of environmental legislation.

Constructed Senate: Committee Negotiations

The Committee on Environmental Affairs spent considerable time working on the details of the Clean Air Act. In this dialogue, Jesse read from his legislation "Reducing Smokestack Pollution."

Jesse: This bill will establish a group of inspectors to go to the plants once a month to make sure the law is being obeyed.

Tom: That's a lot—once a month.

Jesse: (*looking at members of the committee*) Should I say every two months?

Tom: What about every three months, or every two months until the filter is properly used?

Mary: No, because then they should check to make sure the filter has been properly installed and is being used.

Jesse: Yeah, exactly.

Tom: (*nods his head in agreement*)

Mary: So, once every two months.

Jesse: (*changes his original sentence to "once every two months"*)

As can be seen from the dialogue above, the Committee on Environmental Affairs took time considering and negotiating ideas from individual bills. Compromises were struck along the way. For instance, they devised an internal procedure within the bill (e.g., inspections once every two months) to ensure compliance with this proposed law.

Students become inspired when ideas began to build upon one another in committee. The following dialogue shows how Jesse sought to finance the salaries of the inspectors.

Constructed Senate: Building Upon Ideas

The Environmental Affairs Committee determined that revenue collected from fines would help defray the cost of onsite inspections.

Jesse: Wait! (*excited tone*) I know—the money from the fines could be used to pay the inspectors!

Mary: Yes, that's good.

Tom: Okay, so include this as a provision and read it again.

Jesse: Provision Number Five: If a company is fined, the money will go to paying this group of inspectors.

By the end of the week, this committee had constructed a comprehensive bill entitled "Clean Air." It included eight separate provisions. For details of this bill, see Resource I.

The Environmental Affairs Committee validated and appraised the ideas of its members. They worked carefully and examined their own drafts of individual legislation as a way to further improve the Clean Air Act. While it began as Mary's bill, it was soon embraced as the committee's bill. Tom commented upon this process.

> It took a long time thinking about it and deciding what to do in writing it. That was probably the biggest part. 'Cause we actually think that our bill is pretty good. It is well thought out. I like the way we really were involved in it.

From working in committee, Tom understood that the process of creating legislation took a long time. He valued this work because it was "well thought out." This was a notable comment from Tom. Throughout the year, he had developed a pattern of completing his academic work in a hurried fashion. In this context, however, Tom was markedly different. Working with his peers, he was more deliberate in the way he was engaged in his work. He was now paying attention to detail.

As students are actively engaging in the construction process of this curriculum drama, we need as teachers to become genuinely open to their involvement in and ownership of this endeavor. Based on our active observations of their legislative activities, we are then able to work alongside them, and at times we suffer along with them! Being reflective practitioners, we are constantly thinking about our own position within this setting. When should we advise? Question? Listen? Walk away?

Constructed Senate: Prioritized Legislation

In our constructed senate, each of the five committees met deadline and developed prioritized legislation.

Committee	Legislation
Economic Development and Energy	Living wage jobs for the unemployed
Education	HIV/AIDS curriculum
Environmental Affairs	Clean air
Family and Health	Gay marriage and adoption
Security and Immigration	Reducing crime by increasing police presence in major cities

---

Summary

Students began to take ownership of this senate experience by engaging in different tasks (e.g., devising legislation, appraising legislative ideas, writing letters) and participating in various settings (e.g., official senate sessions, committee meetings). This helped to develop multiple layers of allegiance within the senate, and it strengthened the autonomy and commitment toward the work of the classroom senate. At the same time, class meetings were held to guide students about pertinent procedures and terms that related to their current legislative practice.

Through the building of community and their engagement within it, students became part of a bigger identity than who they were as individual senators. Through collaborations in committee, students enacted the power of collective action and effort. By so doing, they projected themselves and generated multiple solutions and pathways to issues. This enabled students, for the most part, to "set aside familiar distinctions and definitions" (Greene, 1995, p. 3) that they might have had as an individual voice, and instead to align themselves in pursuing a common goal—prioritized legislation.

What's Next?

Chapter 7 explores the construction of legislative hearings. Two hearings are described. One hearing examines a crime bill entitled S 121 "Reducing Crime," and the other examines an environmental bill entitled S 125 "Clean Air." Through the task of listening to and questioning witness testimony, students as senators grapple with the complexities involved in legislative initiatives.

7

Constructing a Hearing

Appraising Witness Testimony

Curriculum drama uses as a key resource the diverse range of interests and life experiences within the classroom. For instance, the previous chapter described how students crafted legislation from their own understandings about the world. Working in committee, students decided legislative priorities.

This chapter describes the process of building a witness list and constructing a hearing for legislation that has been prioritized by the senate. Table 7.1 outlines the plan of action during this phase of the classroom senate.

The final segment of this chapter, "Curriculum Drama in Action: Witness Testimony," explores the unexpected world of legislative hearings. Using my own constructed senate as a backdrop, I explore one situation where there was a breakdown in belief and another where there was a building of belief. Why were the two experiences so different? What lessons can we learn about constructing a viable hearing experience?

Classroom Practice: Constructing a Hearing

Whether your class is studying ancient civilizations, modern history, or current events, transform a class session to a formal hearing and bring social studies to life. Invite witnesses to testify about their roles in a defined event. This chapter provides interesting ideas and activities for transforming a class to a formal hearing and helping students (and teachers) construct credible roles as witnesses.

Table 7.1 Plan of Action: Constructing a Hearing

Topic	Situation	Sessions
Prioritizing Legislation		2
Becoming acquainted with prioritized legislation	Class activity	
Class meeting	Student/teacher negotiations	
Setting the Stage		3
Creating a witness list	Student/teacher negotiations	
Locating witnesses to testify	Student/teacher negotiations	
Preparing witnesses	Teacher briefs the witnesses	
Witness Testimony	Event: Legislative hearing	2
Transforming the classroom environment to a legislative hearing		

Prioritizing Legislation

By this point in the classroom drama, students have followed their legislation into committee and have worked with others to develop a prioritized bill (see Chapter 6 for details). The following lists the sequence of committee-related activities that has taken place so far in the classroom senate.

1. Each senator writes a bill.

2. Each bill goes into committee, and the senators follow their bills into the assigned committee.

3. Each committee prioritizes one bill.

At this juncture, the senate is now in the position to determine which of these committees will be the first to hold a legislative *hearing* on its prioritized bill. The following lists the next steps.

1. The senate selects a bill from the prioritized legislation emerging from each committee.

2. The senate constructs a witness list for that bill.

3. The senate conducts a legislative hearing on that bill.

Political Terminology

Hearing: A meeting—usually public—of a committee to take testimony from a witness. Committee members probe testimony so they can develop deeper understandings about their bill and recommend subsequent action on it (e.g., revisions, additional provisions).

SOURCE: Virtual Reference Desk at http://www.senate.gov

Becoming Acquainted With Prioritized Legislation

To ensure that all members of the senate have read the particulars of each committee's bill, post the legislation in a prominent place on a classroom wall, and allow time for students to read these prioritized bills. Students can post a reflective comment next to each committee's legislation.

Extension: Introducing Prioritized Legislation to the Senate

Make it an event! Which committee's bill deserves to be placed first on the senate's calendar? Have a senate leader conduct a full senate session on this issue. Each committee chairperson can read the entire text of the committee's prioritized legislation. Senators can make impromptu public statements (or deliver prepared speeches) in support of particular legislation.

Class Meeting

Hold a class meeting to discuss the process for selecting which bill the senate should review first. As the U.S. Constitution does not offer guidance with this issue, the class needs to agree upon a process. Should one person make this decision or should more people be involved? If this is a full senate session, should decisions be made by public vote or secret ballot? Table 7.2 provides options for the class to consider.

This is a pivotal moment with the classroom senate. The legislation that is chosen will move the committee experience to a formal hearing. Does the full senate want to participate in making this

Table 7.2   Who Makes the Decision About Legislative Priority?

Potential Decision Makers	People Involved in Decision-Making Process
President Pro Tempore	1
Majority Party	More than half the class
Full Senate	Entire class

decision or do they want one person (president pro tempore) or selected people (party leadership) to decide? This experience could even lead the class to a discussion about direct and representative democracy.

Shortcut

No time for students to engage in decision making? Use your authority as the teacher to select the bill. Explain your reasons to the class on why this legislation has been given top priority.

Constructed Senate: Prioritized Legislation

In our classroom senate, the president pro tempore, with advice from the majority and minority party leaders, examined five prioritized bills. The first legislation that the senate addressed was the bill entitled S 121, "Reducing Crime"; it came from the Committee on Security and Immigration. The second legislation was entitled S 125, "Clean Air"; it came from the Environmental Affairs Committee. Both bills received hearings and were subsequently debated. The other prioritized bills remained in committee.

Setting the Stage

Congress invites testimony from a variety of people in a legislative hearing so as to develop a deeper understanding about the potential impact of proposed legislation. Testimony from various individuals provides an opportunity to hear multiple viewpoints. Some may provide supportive testimony and others may provide critical testimony about the bill. Still others may support one part of the legislation while at the same time expressing opposition to another part of it.

Witness testimony provides a platform for close review of the legislation. Through this process, the committee becomes well acquainted with the bill's possible benefits and potential limitations. In a subsequent markup session, the committee further develops the legislation based on the issues that were brought forward in the hearing.

Creating a Witness List

Once the senate has determined the first piece of legislation that will enter a hearing phase, work with the class to create a witness list. Think broadly about the legislation. Which groups of people are likely to be strong supporters of this legislation? What objections or concerns might other segments of the population have about this bill? Challenge students to think about how some individuals might have mixed views about the legislation, supporting some elements of it but opposing other parts.

Constructed Senate: Creating a Witness List—Private Citizen to Public Expert

Over the years various witnesses have testified at our senate hearings. In the event that we were unable to get bona fide witnesses, the class or members of the school community constructed the characters. Here is a sample list describing witnesses and how their expertise connected to the legislation under scrutiny.

Witnesses	Legislation	Rationale
❏ An elderly citizen who lives in a high crime area (This is a constructed witness; the student crafted her character based on her grandmother's experiences.)	S 121, "Reducing Crime"	Personal testimony supports one aspect of the bill—the need for public safety—while arguing against its proposed funding source (cuts to health care funding).
❏ A criminologist who has published research on urban environments, youth and crime (This is a bona fide witness! The criminologist was a class parent.)		Expert testimony provides current research detailing studies that support a key aspect of this bill—the need for community youth centers.
❏ A coal miner who lost his job when his mine was shut down due to the high cost of environmental safeguards (This is a constructed witness; the student crafted her testimony based on a newspaper article).	S 125, "Clean Air"	Personal testimony provides a critique on the high cost of environmental safeguards.
❏ A chemist who supports clean air. (This is a constructed witness; a math teacher constructed this testimony based on personal experiences and extensive readings.)		Expert testimony provides scientific research detailing support for various aspects within this legislation.

(Continued)

(Continued)

The hearing experience works best when credible witnesses reflect a wide array of positions about the bill. These individuals can provide informed perspectives based on their personal life experiences or their professional expertise.

Locating Witnesses to Testify

Once the class has brainstormed a list containing four to six people with a broad range of informed viewpoints, experiences, and expertise, begin the process of locating these witnesses. This is easier than it might seem.

Begin by identifying local experts who might be available to testify. Ideally, these can be solicited from among students' and parents' contacts. Most likely, however, experts are busy and in high demand. Fortunately, schools are a wonderful source for witnesses! Work with the class to determine who on the faculty or staff might be receptive to the challenge of constructing witness roles.

Using your position as teacher (or as senate clerk), make contact with possible witnesses. To help prepare witnesses for the hearing, provide them with copies of the prioritized bill and a sample of an opening statement (see Resource L).

Tapping School Resources for Expert Testimony

Invite members of the school community to testify as expert witnesses. In their respective jobs and outside interests, there is a considerable range of expertise.

Legislative Topics	Witnesses Drawn From the School Community
Health Care	School nurse, counselors
Food Safety	Cafeteria staff
School Safety	Security staff, maintenance staff
Sports	Coach, gym teacher

Don't forget to tap into the parent body of your class. Local community workers (e.g., police, postal workers) can provide another source of potential witnesses.

A bill may emerge from the classroom senate that presents the perfect opportunity for someone within the school community to testify from a perspective grounded in firsthand experience or from related professional expertise. Not only does this situation bring the world into the classroom, thereby enriching the senate experience, but it also communicates a powerful message about how members of the school community support classroom endeavors.

Constructing the Role: Adult as Witness

In the event that the class calls for witnesses with specialized expertise, it might be necessary for adults as witnesses to construct these roles. Which adults in the school community will be receptive to this challenge? Elicit ideas from your students. Who would they like to invite, who would you like to invite? Which adults will have the time to prepare their testimony and write an informed opening statement for the hearing? Another issue for the class to decide is whether adults should be given scripted roles with predetermined perspectives or be given the freedom to construct their own roles based on a loose frame of reference. While it requires a certain degree of time, inquiry, and imagination to become another, colleagues are often honored by the opportunity to draw from their background readings, life experiences, or personal interests to develop credible testimony in their constructed roles.

Constructing the Role: Student as Witness

Students can also construct witness roles. Drawing from their own background readings and life experiences, students as witnesses can provide insightful and thoughtful testimony in a legislative hearing. Students who have constructed roles as senators *and* as witnesses have *double roles*. When it is time to testify as a witness, the student as senator leaves the room and returns as a witness. Once the testimony is over, the witness then exits the room and returns moments later as a senator.

> **Double Role**
>
> This occurs when an individual temporarily leaves his or her primary role within the curriculum drama and constructs another role.

Sometimes students decide to construct a role based on their deep understanding of persons in their lives. This was the case with Katie. When the committee decided that they wanted to hear testimony from a senior citizen, Katie immediately volunteered. She constructed her opening statement based on her grandmother's situation. In her role as Mrs. Fay Michaels, Katie did not attempt to act like her grandmother. She did not use props, change her voice, alter her posture, or adjust her attire. Instead, when responding to questions posed during the hearing, she focused her efforts on considering her grandmother's perspective and portraying her grandmother's position on various provisions within the legislation.

**Constructed Senate: Opening
Statement From a Student as Witness**

The Security and Immigration Committee held a hearing on S 121, "Reducing Crime." They invited Mrs. Fay Michaels, a senior citizen, to testify.

I am a housewife. My husband is retired and we live in Miami. We do not live in a retirement home; we live in the house we bought several years ago. Over the years, we have witnessed an increase in crime, and this makes us nervous. We think twice about going to the corner store for milk and eggs at night. So in a sense, I support the bill "Reducing Crime." We need more police, and they need to be better paid. We also need more youth centers where teenagers can hang out. So I support this part of the bill.

On the other hand, however, I have a lot of medical expenses. So does my husband. I don't approve of your taking from the federal Medicaid budget to pay for this security measure. Being retired, we don't have that much money, and we worry a lot about health care expenses. . . .

Katie as Mrs. Fay Michaels testified against the funding mechanism of this bill. In her role as a senior citizen, she expressed credible concern about the bill's impact on her health needs.

Interestingly, Katie was a member of the Security and Immigration Committee, and she actually supported this legislation. In fact, it was her idea to obtain funding for this legislation from the health care budget! During the course of committee research on this bill, she noted how the Department of Health and Human Services had one of the highest reported federal budgets.

Word of Advice: Taking Positions in Role

To avoid possible misunderstandings, make it clear to the class that when people construct their positions as witnesses, they are given license to take on the role of a person different from who they actually are. The perspective expressed by the witness is not necessarily the same perspective as that of the individual who is portraying that role.

Preparing Witnesses

In the days before the hearing, make contact with those individuals who have been identified by your class as viable witnesses. Orient these individuals (e.g., via e-mail, phone, hallway conversations) to the classroom senate experience. Along with confirming the date and time of their arrival at the classroom senate, provide them with copies of the prioritized legislation. Review with them the format and structure of the hearing, so they know what to expect. Consider the following order of events for each witness session:

- Committee chairperson gives welcoming remarks.
- Witness gives opening statement.
- Committee poses relevant questions to the witness.
- Other members of the senate pose relevant questions to the witness.
- Committee chairperson thanks the witness.

Advise witnesses to prepare written opening statements ahead of time. Ideally, the class should be able to review these statements before the hearing, so as to craft relevant questions to the witness. The opening statement, written in the first person, essentially contains four elements:

1. Introductory statement—background of the witness (*identifies the individual in some way: full name, home state, marital status, occupation, military service, etc.*)

2. Witness's connection to this bill (*related expertise or life experience*)

3. Impact that the witness anticipates this bill as law will have on the nation (*includes evidence to support this position*)

4. Concluding statement (*encourages passage or defeat of bill, suggests ways to improve or change the bill*)

Constructed Senate: Opening
Statement From an Adult as Witness

The Environmental Affairs Committee invited Mr. Wilk, an environmental educator, to testify. In the school setting, he is a science teacher. Here is an excerpt from his testimony:

(Continued)

(Continued)

I have been working as an environmental educator for the past ten years. . . . I am pleased to testify today in support of the proposed Clean Air Act. As an advocate for children's rights and healthy environments for people to live in, I am especially pleased to see that your bill directly addresses one of the most critical aspects of air quality: particulate matter from the exhaust of diesel engines and coal- or oil-fired furnaces. . . .

While the cost associated with the implementation and enforcement of this bill will be significant, it is a sound investment in the future of our national health. . . .

As an environmentalist in real life, this witness provided testimony that tapped into his own experience and professional expertise.

Points of Comparison

Preparing for a legislative hearing provides a natural place to compare the classroom senate to the U.S. Senate. Table 7.3 compares the legislative hearing at these two sites.

Table 7.3   Points of Comparison: Comparing Legislative Hearings

	Classroom Senate	U.S. Senate
Chairperson	Yes	Yes
Number of Hearings at One Time	One	Several
Witness Testimony	Yes	Yes
Participants	All	Only committee members may pose questions to the witness

Within the classroom senate, there is only one hearing that is scheduled at a time. In contrast, the U.S. Senate runs multiple hearings simultaneously. Another difference in the two hearings is the participation factor. In the classroom context, committee members along with the other senators may pose questions to the witness. In the U.S. Senate, only the members of the respective committee may pose questions to a witness testifying at a given hearing.

Extension: Seeing a Hearing in Action

Before the class engages in their own hearing, provide time in the classroom (or for homework) to watch a televised U.S. Senate hearing. What patterns do students notice about the sort of questions that legislators pose to various witnesses? What makes for a good question? What makes for a credible witness? For compelling testimony?

For a field trip experience during school hours or as an after school civic-related activity, plan a class trip to a public hearing at the town hall, school board, or community council.

Witness Testimony: An Event

As a way to further belief in the constructed experience of the hearing, align the structure of the classroom to that of a hearing, and bring in objects that can serve as tools of the trade for this event.

Transforming the Classroom Environment to a Legislative Hearing

Rearrange classroom furniture to resemble the way tables and chairs are organized for a hearing. Position the committee's table in the front of the room. Place the witness table a short distance from the committee. The witness table and the committee table should face one another. Adjacent to the committee table on either side, arrange the seats for the Republicans and the Democrats. Figure 7.1 illustrates the classroom environment for a legislative hearing.

Figure 7.1   Formal Hearing: Classroom Arrangement

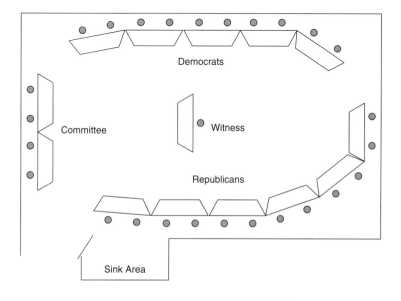

Tools of the Trade

Along with reconfiguring the room to accommodate witness testimony, the appearance of the following objects provides a signal that the classroom is now poised to enter formal hearing mode.

Place individual desk cards at all seating areas. Those who are senators will have their senate names in public view. Those who are witnesses will have desk cards with honorific titles before their constructed names (e.g., Ms., Mr., Prof., Dr., Rev.) or acronyms indicating positions of power (e.g., CEO). Perhaps certain cards could even indicate the witness's academic achievement (e.g., MBA, JD, PhD). These cards serve to remind participants about their respective positions. In addition, these cards help to set a formal tone for this senate session.

Use a gavel to signal the start and conclusion of a committee's session in a hearing.

Use written testimony: Senators should have accessible their own copies of the witness's opening statement and the questions they intend to ask this witness.

Place current copies of the prioritized legislation at all seating areas.

Use a pitcher of water: As a courtesy to the witness, there is a pitcher of water and a glass on the witness table. A designated committee member could solicitously pour water in the witness's drinking glass before the hearing proceeds.

Curriculum Drama in Action: Witness Testimony

This section explores two hearings that took place within our constructed senate. The Security and Immigration Committee conducted a hearing on S 121, "Reducing Crime," and heard testimony from four witnesses. One of these witnesses was Dr. Van Schick, a heart surgeon; a student, Greg had constructed this role. In this particular session, credibility in the senate stuttered and then stalled.

A few weeks later, the Environmental Affairs Committee conducted a hearing on its bill, S 125, "Clean Air," and heard testimony from four witnesses. One of these witnesses was Will Cart, a foreman in a West Virginia mine; a student, Amanda, had constructed this role.

This experience informed the senate; senators used findings from Mr. Cart's testimony to question subsequent witnesses who came to testify.

Why the difference in these two experiences? What lessons can we learn from each?

S 121, "Reducing Crime": Testimony From a Heart Surgeon

The Security and Immigration Committee heard two days of testimony on their prioritized legislation, "Reducing Crime." The goal of this bill was to create a surge in police activity in high-crime areas around the nation. Along with increasing police salaries and training, it also sought to create additional youth centers. Funding for this initiative came from the health care budget. Details of this bill are located in Resource J.

On the second day of the hearing, the senate heard testimony from Greg as Dr. Van Schick. Resource K contains his public statement. In his opening remarks, the doctor sought to convey the idea that while it made sense to have additional police in high-crime areas, he did not want the money to come out of the federal health care budget.

In the back and forth between the witness and the senator, hilarity ensued, and the constructed legislative world was temporarily abandoned.

Constructed Senate: Hearing on S 121, "Reducing Crime"

Sen. Fox (Jill), chairperson of the committee, greeted Dr. Van Schick (Greg) at the classroom door and led him to his seat in the center of the room.

Sen. Fox: (Jill)	Welcome, Dr. Van Schick. Thank you for arranging your schedule to come to our hearing on S 121 "Reducing Crime." We are ready to hear your opening statement. Please proceed.
Dr. Van Schick: (Greg)	*(After reading his testimony, Dr. Van Schick paused and waited for questions.)*
Sen. Fox: (Jill)	Does the committee have any questions for Dr. Van Schick?
Sen. Belt: (Bill)	Dr. Van Schick, when you do your average surgery, what does that usually cost the patient?

(Continued)

(Continued)	
Dr. Van Schick: (Greg)	(*shrugs*) It depends on the type of surgery.
Sen. Belt: (Bill)	The average?
Dr. Van Schick: (Greg)	Well, there is no average surgery.
Sen. Belt: (Bill)	(*smiling*) Consider the cost of every surgery you have done and add them together. Divide this figure by the number of surgeries that you have done; about what would that come out to?
Dr. Van Schick: (Greg)	(*looking around with a grin and sighing*) I couldn't answer that.
Sen. Belt: (Bill)	(*sustained pause*) Approximately?
Dr. Van Schick: (Greg)	(*sustained pause, suppressing laughter with visible difficulty*) . . . hmmm . . . $8,000? . . . (*begins laughing uncontrollably*)

At this point, Senator Belt, persistent and unflappable in his line of questioning, realized in shock that the witness was unable to proceed. Dr. Van Schick had collapsed in unbridled laughter and was hunched down at the witness table with his head covered by his arms. Members of the senate recognized the hilarity of the moment and they joined in with good-natured laughter. The experience had turned into comedy!

Classroom Dilemma: Rupture of Credibility

Unlike the certainty and structure of a textbook driven lesson, curriculum drama has an underlying current of unpredictability. This approach relies on a sustained and collective belief that the constructed world within the classroom is possible and even pertinent. Its credibility deepens through the use of collaborative imagination and active inquiry; students construct new frames of reference and interact in new and convincing ways with one another. There are times, however, when this does not happen. As the teacher, what do you do?

Dilemmas as Fuel for Discussions

Dilemmas that emerge in curriculum drama provide rich material for class discussions. Why did students break from this experience? In the debriefing session, refer back to the witnesses or senators by the names they used in the constructed senate, not by the actual names of the individuals who had been interacting within that position. In this way, the class can reflect upon the senate experience with a certain degree of linguistic distance. The goal of this session is not to cast blame on any individual. Nor is the purpose of this session necessarily to resolve the issue of senate credibility. Instead the aim is to create space for a range of views to analyze this collective experience.

Constructed Senate: Discussing the Experience

In a discussion about our legislative hearing, students noted a difference between the first and second days of testimony. I, "Catherine," began the discussion with the following open ended question:

Catherine: The Security and Immigration Committee has had two days of testimony now on their bill S 121, "Reducing Crime." So what do you think about these sessions?

Sue: Mrs. Fay Michaels was probably the most believable witness we have heard so far, because she was a real person.

Catherine: What do you mean, "She was a real person"?

Sue: Well, Mrs. Fay Michaels was Katie's grandmother, and so Katie had an idea of how to portray a senior citizen's perspective. Her testimony was based on her grandmother, a real person.

Amanda: Yeah. Good point. Yesterday's witness was not based on a real doctor. And even if he had been, even if that was an **actual doctor** (*bolded for spoken emphasis*), so what? His testimony, especially when he attempted to answer questions related to surgery costs, was a complete joke. Did we really need to know the average cost of surgery?

Catherine: What reasons could Sen. Belt have for posing that question? Why was it a challenge for Dr. Van Schick to respond to that question?

By listening to students' comments and posing follow-up questions, we began to tease out the difference between the two days of testimony. For instance, we noted how the first day's testimony was constructed based on the deep understandings of an individual and her life experiences. In this instance, Katie could readily envision her grandmother, Mrs. Fay Michael, and in doing so, she was able to create credible testimony. In contrast, the second day's testimony was constructed from a composite image. While Greg knew about medical doctors from his own general life experiences, his deep understandings were actually limited. Upon responding to persistent questions from one senator, Greg could not maintain a credible portrayal of his constructed witness, Dr. Van Schick. Unlike Katie, who could frame her responses based on her recent conversations with her grandmother, Greg was at a disadvantage.

Guidelines for Future Hearings

Situational missteps in curriculum drama provide valuable material for class discussions and teacher reflections. Together the students and I created simple guidelines for future hearings.

> Witness: Witness roles should be based on personal experience, expertise, and/or background research. In the event that a person has constructed a witness role, this role needs to be taken seriously and portrayed in a credible way. Individuals should avoid constructing witness roles based on fantasy or stereotypes.

> Opening Statement: The witness needs to include information (e.g., facts, informed perspective) that will help the senate understand the legislation in a new way.

> Testimony: If a witness cannot answer a senator's question or does not understand a senator's question, the witness can say "I don't know" or "I don't have the answer readily available, but I will find out and get back to you." This is better than making up an answer. Witnesses are not expected to know all the answers.

> Questions: Senators need to pose questions that relate directly to the legislation and to the witness. Furthermore, the senate needs to remember that the witness is not on trial; rather, the witness is doing a civic duty by providing informed testimony.

S 125 "Clean Air": Testimony
From Two Coal Miners

The Environmental Affairs Committee arranged a legislative hearing on S 125, "Clean Air"; see Resource I for details on this bill. While we had guidelines from the previous hearing to help us with witness role constructions and crafting questions, I decided to create a team research session to explore library and Web resources on reported issues that were relevant to this legislation. This helped to develop collective understanding of relevant issues connected to this bill. In addition, this research session helped fuel the task of creating a witness list.

Research Session

I divided the class into three groups, and each met at a separate location within the library. Pairs of students researched material from periodicals, journals, and reference sources that connected in some way to the Clean Air Act. One group read material that I had obtained about the health benefits and economic costs of environmental legislation. Another group used the library's computers to search databases (e.g., LexisNexis) for news articles related to clean air legislation. A third group explored the library's catalog for books and other reference sources on this issue.

At the end of this session, each research team reported what their findings were and what reference sources they had used. Two students, Amanda and Mike, were particularly excited about their research work. In looking at back issues of the *New York Times,* they located an article critical of the 1990 Clean Air Act. As a result of tighter environmental standards, 1,000 coal mines had closed in West Virginia (Kilborn, 1996). They decided that they wanted to represent the interests of coal miners at the upcoming hearing.

Amanda and Mike then asked the members of the Environmental Affairs Committee for permission to construct witness roles as coal miners. Knowing in advance that this testimony would be highly critical of the legislation, the committee judiciously agreed to this idea.

Teacher Dilemma

While I was delighted with the initiative of the two students who sought to portray the interests of coal miners, I was concerned about their ability to provide informed testimony. I did not want a repeat performance of a witness collapsing into laughter. If a student had difficulty portraying a medical doctor—an individual in a career that most were familiar with either from life experience or from television programs, how could students meaningfully portray the interests of coal miners? Neither Amanda nor Mike had ever met coal miners, or had been in a coal mining community. How could they portray the concerns of people they did not know?

On the other hand, both Amanda and Mike had gathered background information from a news article on which to ground their testimony. They knew that they could weave the reported details from the article into their statements to the committee. Then too, they planned to testify as a team, not individually—so they could easily consult with one another in the event that they got stumped by a question posed to them at the hearing. They prepared their opening statements and used their close reading of the news article and their powers of imagination to convey the respective experiences of two individuals who had lost their jobs at a coal mine due to mandated environmental regulations.

Constructed Senate: Testimony From West Virginian Coal Miners

After they finished reading their prepared statements (see Resource L), "Mr. Cart" (Amanda) and "Mr. McCrag" (Mike) responded to a comment made by a senator from the Environmental Affairs Committee.

Sen. Wright: (Tom)	First of all, I would like to remind you that our bill was not passed in 1990, and it is not the Clean Air Act that you are referring to. Your concerns about our bill are not relevant.
Mr. Cart: (Amanda)	I respectfully disagree. It is similar to the Clean Air Act. In reading your bill it states that you have to have filters, and these filters are relevant. They cost $100 million and up. . . .
Sen. Wright: (Tom)	But it is tax deductible.
Mr. Cart: (Amanda)	But that doesn't matter. **It is $100 million and up!** (*bolded to emphasize agitated tone of voice*)
Mr. McCrag: (Mike)	It is a lot of money.
Mr. Cart: (Amanda)	We obviously don't want air pollution. If there is a way to reduce it, we want to do so, but without having us all lose our jobs.

Amanda was intensely engaged in her spoken portrayal of Mr. Cart, an unemployed West Virginian coal miner. She skillfully used facts drawn from background reading to prepare her opening statement (Resource L) and to fuel her responses to questions posed by Sen. Wright. Despite the fact that she did not have any personal life connections to the coal mining industry, she was nonetheless credible in her role. She offered compelling testimony about how a concerned citizen had suffered economic hardship as an indirect result of federal regulations. Furthermore, as evidenced by the increasing level of exasperation in her voice, she revealed the extent to which she was connecting to her constructed role as a witness.

Through the stories of Mr. Cart and Mr. McCrag, and the corresponding statements and questions posed by senators, students confronted the inherent complexities of environmental regulations. This preliminary session set the tone for subsequent testimonies. Students developed an ease for analyzing and questioning witnesses. In doing so, they explored issues related to short-term expenses (e.g., filter costs) and long-term health benefits connected to this legislation.

Constructed Senate: Learning From Experience

In this second legislative hearing, I had made adjustments in setting the stage for this experience.

- Before the legislative hearing began, the class conducted research on issues related to the legislation.
- Readings from their committee research session helped students to trigger ideas for a witness list.
- Students as witnesses testified as a team.
- Student testimony was inspired from published news articles.

Amanda and Mike were the only students who volunteered to become witnesses in the Clean Air hearing. The committee had determined that they also wanted testimony from a worker at a chemical processing plant, an environmental scientist, and a city bus driver. With approval from the committee, I enlisted the support of colleagues at the school. A couple of teachers agreed to review the students' environmental legislation and to prepare statements that reflected the experience base and perspective of these three witnesses.

**Constructed Senate: Testimony From
a Worker in a Chemical Processing Plant**

In this legislative hearing, "Mrs. Leaf" is a worker in a chemical processing plant. In the school setting, she is a math teacher.

Sen. Cape: **(Jim)**	This bill will require companies to buy filters, which are quite expensive. Currently, they cost $100 million. Your company might try to save money and cut back on labor costs. Aren't you worried that you will then lose your job?
Mrs. Leaf:	Sure, I'm worried about losing my job, but . . . I'm more worried about the effect that pollution has on the environment.
Sen. Blitz: **(Mike)**	A lot of people like the clean air idea, but they will be losing their jobs.
Mrs. Leaf:	Well, I think it is the government's responsibility to help smaller companies stay in business.
Sen. Blitz: **(Mike)**	To help these companies costs a lot of money. It is many millions of dollars . . . the government is going to have to pay a lot of money.

As may be noted, Mike had a double role; he had played the role of a coal miner in the previous day's testimony. In this session, Mike as Senator Blitz used his previous day's witness testimony to frame comments back to Mrs. Leaf (e.g., "The government is going to have to pay a lot of money").

Following the testimony of Mrs. Leaf, the senators invited a witness who had expertise on environmental education to testify. Once again, they used the testimony from the coal miners to pose cost related questions.

**Constructed Senate: Testimony From
an Expert Witness—Environmental Educator**

In this legislative hearing, "Mr. Wilk" is an environmental educator. His prepared statement to the committee appears earlier in this chapter.

Sen. Mix: **(Kate)**	We heard testimony the other day about the cost of chimney filters. As you may know, this technology is designed to filter out the bad air from pollution-causing smoke stacks. What do you think is an appropriate cost of a filter?

Mr. Wilk:	Well, since we live in a free market society, it is what the market will bear.
Sen. Mix: (Kate)	Well, right now they are selling for $100 million. . . . Not many factories can purchase these, because the price is so high.

In both of these sessions, it was the students as senators who were informing the adults as witnesses about the high price tag for using the latest environmental safeguards to filter the air. Introduced in earlier testimony by coal miners, the $100 million cost for scrubbers became the prevailing issue with this legislation. Despite subsequent testimony that was strongly supportive of the Clean Air Act, the senate became increasingly preoccupied with the economic impact of mandating costly filters.

While the students were respectful of the adults' testimonies and their perspectives on the legislation, they did not necessarily accept it at face value. In fact, they probed testimony from different angles and from different points of view. Students even went beyond asking questions; they also commented upon adult testimony and in some cases disputed it. This was a reversal from the conventional classroom situation. In this case, it was the students driving the content of the curriculum. They were informing the adults-as-witnesses about findings from prior testimony.

Of course, not everyone asked questions; most in fact listened. Nonetheless in their decision to listen carefully to the proceedings, they showed in nonverbal ways that the discourse between witness and senators was both relevant and meaningful.

Moreover, their collective attention to the dialogue added an additional layer of believability to the situation. At moments when they had private conversations with peers, they spoke quietly and briefly. For the most part, the exchange of ideas between the witnesses and the senators held their attention and curiosity.

Summary

Once it is in action, the constructed hearing created a situation where students took charge and appraised witness testimony on legislation. While the first hearing on S 121, "Reducing Crime," was problematic, the second hearing on S 125, "Clean Air," was highly productive. Students as coal miners constructed testimony that became the pivotal point of inquiry in the legislative hearing.

What's Next?

Chapter 8 explores the process of setting the stage for senate debate and legislative action. Through the task of engaging in the full scope of legislative practice, students develop skill, experience, and deep understandings about the legislative branch of government.

8

Constructing a Debate

Taking Legislative Action

Curriculum drama triggers situations within the classroom where students are positioned to develop understanding within the content area itself. For instance, the previous chapter described how students constructed hearings for two pieces of legislation. Through the back and forth of witness testimony and committee questions, students as senators appraised S 121, "Reducing Crime," and S 125, "Clean Air."

This chapter explores the process of constructing a formal senate debate around legislation. In this situation, student participation drives the experience and determines the fate of the legislation under review. Table 8.1 outlines the plan of action during this phase of the classroom senate.

The final segment of this chapter, "Curriculum Drama in Action: Senate Debate," explores the unpredictable world of legislation when it enters this final stage of official consideration. Using events that occurred within our constructed senate, I describe the debate of S 121, "Reducing Crime," and the committee's subsequent decision during their markup session. I then describe the debate of S 125, "Clean Air," and the flurry of activity when debate ended and the voting process was about to begin.

Table 8.1   Plan of Action: Constructing a Debate

Topic	Situation	Session
Committee Decision	Committee work	1

Setting the Stage
    Forming guidelines for senate debate
    Using the language of the senate
    Introducing strategic procedures
	Class meeting	2

Senate Debate	Event	1

**Classroom Practice:
Constructing a Debate**

In your social studies classroom, do you use debate as a way for students to grapple in a public way with a particular topic? How do you ensure that students participate with both vigor and informed understanding? This chapter provides suggestions for transforming the classroom into a formal debate setting.

Committee Decision

After completion of the hearing process (see Chapter 7), the committee might want to mark up the bill to address prevailing issues that surfaced during witness testimony. After this revision process, the committee then distributes the latest version of the legislation to the senate. After debate, the committee has another opportunity to mark up the bill before it is scheduled for a senate vote.

Setting the Stage

In the days before the scheduled debate, engage the class in a series of activities to prepare them for the upcoming senate session.

Forming Guidelines for Senate Debate

So as to ensure an orderly debate process, discuss with students the characteristics of an effective debate. What has been their experience with classroom debates in the past?

Explore the U.S. Constitution with the class to determine if there are any guidelines for holding a senate debate. Direct their attention to this line from Article 1, section 8:

Each house may determine the rules of its proceedings.

Working in their committees, invite students to devise guidelines for their upcoming debate. Have each committee present and discuss its ideas before the entire class. Post each committee's recommended guidelines in the classroom. Have the class vote by secret ballot on those ideas that will help them to conduct an orderly and informed debate.

Constructed Senate: Guidelines for Senate Debate

In our senate, students decided upon these guidelines for their upcoming senate debate:

- ❏ A designated leader will facilitate the debate in a fair manner.
- ❏ A designated leader will call on individuals who wish to speak by stating, "Senator _____ from the state of _____."
- ❏ Senators who wish to speak will first raise their hands.
- ❏ Senators will wait patiently for their turns to speak publicly.
- ❏ A senator who wishes to speak a second or third time will abide by the "three before me" rule; three individuals will need to speak before this senator may speak another time.

Shortcut

Instead of having students work independently within their committees, hold a class meeting to generate guidelines for senate debate.

Using the Language of the Senate

Conduct a minisession on how senators will refer to one another in a formal setting and how they might express their support of, or disagreement with, a colleague's point of view.

- I agree with Senator Koch, *from the great state of Texas,* because. . . .
- I agree with *my dear colleague and good friend,* Senator Koch, because. . . .
- I *respectfully disagree* with Senator Koch's position on this issue because. . . .
- I *vehemently disagree* with my dear colleague and good friend, Senator Koch, from the great state of Texas, because. . . .

Another phrase to introduce is "yield the floor." Once a senator has stated a position, the individual can then say, "I yield the floor." This alerts the designated leader that another senator can now be recognized.

In the days leading up to the debate, have students practice this language in classroom conversations.

Introducing Strategic Procedures

This is an ideal time to reintroduce the terms *filibuster* and *cloture* (see Chapter 2). For a variety of reasons, senators may want to strategically extend the debate experience so as to filibuster (delay) an anticipated legislative action (e.g., holding a vote). To prevent this from happening, the senate can vote for cloture; this limits debate.

Extension: Watching a Senate Debate

For homework or as a class session, have students watch a televised debate within Congress. What makes for a compelling speech? To what extent are Congressional debates democratic? Substantive? Civil?

Senate Debate: An Event

For the debate, place individual senate desk cards and the most updated version of the legislation at everyone's desk. If possible, adjust the seating arrangement of the room to a square or horseshoe configuration. In this way everyone can be seen and heard. Consider placing the committee whose prioritized bill is being debated in a prominent position within the room; arrange for the members of this committee to sit together. If your senate has constructed political parties (see Chapters 4 and 5), consider placing members of each party at opposite sides of the room. Figure 8.1 provides an example of how one classroom arranged desks for this event.

To help the students step into this legislative debate, create internal procedures that will help them get ready. For instance, a senate leader can begin this session by first reviewing the agreed upon guidelines for debate participation. The committee chairperson can then read the prioritized legislation in its entirety. After these preliminaries, the senate can begin debate.

Extension: Party Caucus Before Senate Debate

Party leaders and whips may want to first meet with their respective groups to discuss the legislation under review and to decide whether the senators want to take a unified position in the debate to support the legislation or to oppose it.

Figure 8.1   Senate Debate: Classroom Arrangement

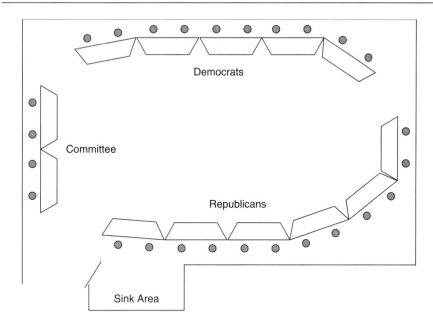

In the event of confusion or disorder, be ready to support the authority of the senate leader. Sometimes it might be necessary to halt proceedings if people forget to abide by the agreed upon guidelines. Sometimes it is necessary to side coach the senate leader and remind him or her to invite the quieter voices to be heard.

Word of Advice: Hearing a Range of Voices in a Senate Debate

To prevent a limited number of speakers from dominating this event, create a temporary break in the situation. Have students cluster together to speak informally with one another about the proceedings. Knowing that their view is shared by others may propel some of the quieter students to speak out when the debate resumes.

Rather than speaking extemporaneously, some students might benefit from reading a statement that they have prepared beforehand that details a position on the bill.

As it was with the legislative hearing, it is impossible to know beforehand how the debate will proceed. While you have coconstructed this experience with your students, and have done considerable work preparing for it, the debate is now in the hands of the senators.

Curriculum Drama in Action: Senate Debate

In the constructed senate, we explored two pieces of prioritized legislation, S 121, "Reducing Crime," and S 125, "Clean Air." For each one we conducted a hearing (see Chapter 7). This section examines the debate experience for both of these bills.

S 121, "Reducing Crime"

In the debate on S 121, "Reducing Crime," the senators began to take notice of how the legislation was designed to benefit selected states and cities. This issue became a major point of contention between committee members and some senators.

Constructed Senate: Debate on S 121, "Reducing Crime"

The senate debated the prioritized legislation that originated within the Security and Immigration Committee. Alex, as Senator Koch, president pro tempore of the senate, facilitated this session. The senators raised a number of questions and concerns to the committee about S 121, "Reducing Crime."

Sen. Koch: (Alex)	Senator East, from the great state of Oklahoma.
Sen. East: (Amanda)	Is this legislation going to be used all across the country or just in states with high crime levels?
Committee:	Well, we are trying to put more police officers where they are needed—the states with the most crime will get the most police officers.
Sen. Vork: (Sue)	I don't understand. In each state, are there going to be the same number of police officers?
Committee:	No.
Sen. Blitz: (Mike)	Senators, this is unfair. I respectfully disagree with the design of this legislation. Why should the federal health care budget be reduced so as to help only certain states with their crime issues?
Committee:	This bill seeks to help troubled spots within our nation, so as a country we will all benefit.
Sen. Blitz: (Mike)	(*rising out of seat and standing to address his colleagues*) For you senators from states with low crime rates, you have nothing to gain from this legislation and much to lose if it passes. My colleagues and good friends on the Security and Immigration Committee are misguided. I do not support this bill as currently designed. I yield the floor.

After this debate, the Security and Immigration Committee met to determine their next course of action. Did they want to work further on this bill? Did they want to bring it to the senate for a vote? The decision was theirs to make.

Classroom Dilemma: Going Along With Student Decisions

The committee notified me that they intended to drop the bill entirely! This caught me by surprise. I thought that the Security and Immigration Committee had planned to use their colleagues' critique as a way to revise their original piece of legislation, S 121, "Reducing Crime." When I met privately with the committee to urge them to reconsider, they were adamant about their decision. In light of the senate debate, they felt there was simply too much opposition to it.

Admittedly, I had mixed feelings with this turn of events. While I was pleased that the legislative process had created a situation where a bill came under collective scrutiny, I was nonetheless disappointed with the bill's outcome. As happens in the U.S. Congress, the bill "died in committee."

Class Discussion

The next time the class met, students heard the news about S 121, "Reducing Crime." The committee had decided not to revise the bill and did not plan to bring it as currently designed to a senate vote. Katie, a committee member, read a prepared statement:

> The Security and Immigration Committee has decided to drop S 121, "Reducing Crime." The testimony presented in the legislative hearing and the arguments expressed in the senate debate made us think more deeply about the bill. As a committee, we have made the decision not to waste taxpayers' money to mark up the bill or to hold a vote on this bill. While we feel that some senators are in favor of it, we believe that at this time more are opposed to it.

The discussion that followed this statement supported the committee's strategic decision. Students mentioned that while they were initially supportive of the bill, their minds changed after listening to varied testimony. Amanda's comment was representative of the class as a whole:

> Well, when I first heard the bill, I thought it was a very good idea. Major cities have crime, and the federal government has to do something about it. Then when the witnesses came up, particularly the senior citizens, I had a different point of view. Hearing the witnesses let me get more opinions and ideas. It sort of let me understand it more.

A few envisioned how this legislation if passed would have an adverse impact on the lives of close family members. For example, Diane formed a position about this bill based on her grandmother's medical needs:

> Well, I was for putting more cops on the streets, but I wasn't for where they were getting the money. 'Cause one of my grandmas, she counts on that money. She has diabetes and she needs to take insulin. She doesn't have a whole lot of money and everything. The bill "Reducing Crime" would have reduced her ability to pay for medicine and had the potential of putting her health care at serious risk.

Collective Decision: Extending the Experience

As we still had time in the semester, we decided to engage in another legislative hearing. We examined S 125, "Clean Air." After listening to the testimony of several witness, we held a debate. My hope was that this bill would move farther along in the senate process than the previous legislation, S 121, "Reducing Crime."

S 125, "Clean Air"

Just as senators noted with concern the funding mechanism of S 121, "Reducing Crime," and the ripple effect it could have on senior citizens, the senators were also concerned about the cost measures connected to S 125, "Clean Air."

Constructed Senate Debate on S 125, "Clean Air"

Alex, as Senator Koch, president pro tempore, facilitated this debate.

Sen. Santos: (Jorge)	I plan to vote for the Clean Air Act. I feel that the nation's air being clean far outweighs the bill's drawbacks. I yield the floor.

Sen. Blitz: (Mike)	I plan on voting against the bill. Although clean air is a great and worthy cause, many people who work in factories will get fired because the factory will need to keep its profit margins up. The filters will cost hundreds of million dollars, and I think that ruining people's lives is not the way to provide clean air. I yield the floor.
Sen. Straus: (Stan)	**I call for a vote.** (*bolded to convey shouting tone*)
Sen. Koch: (Alex)	You can't call for a vote without being recognized.
Sen. Vork: (Sue)	(*calling out*) Well, then recognize him!
Sen. Koch: (Alex)	I have the floor to call on people, and I don't recognize you at this time to speak.

Even in the midst of such pandemonium, senate leadership prevailed. Although challenged by his peers, Alex as Senator Koch managed the flow of debate. Nonetheless, senators became increasingly agitated; it appeared that Senator Koch was recognizing only senators who were aligned to his position on the bill.

Abigail, one of the quieter students in the class, reflected about this moment:

> I felt most like it was a real situation during the harrowing floor debate. I was trying desperately to get a vote on cloture happening. . . . People were really sticking up for their beliefs and battling it out.

Midway in the debate, Senator Koch recognized a senator who made a motion to call for cloture. This motion was seconded and then discussed. Earlier the senate had decided that two-thirds had to agree on cloture and had arrived at 16 as the number of votes required for cloture to go into effect; as a point of comparison, the U.S. Senate requires three-fifths of their senators to agree to this procedural strategy.

By a public show of hands, 16 of the 25 senators indicated their support for cloture. They wanted to begin proceedings to vote for passage of the Clean Air Act. The Environmental Affairs Committee began to smile. Victory was on the near horizon.

At this point a senator who opposed the bill checked the math on cloture and loudly proclaimed that two-thirds of 25 was 17, not 16. On her own accord, she went up to the chalkboard and explained her calculations. This moment was greeted with relief by those who wanted to continue debate.

Teacher Dilemma

As the classroom teacher, I intervened. I felt as though the senate had exhausted the debate experience. Both supporters and opponents of the bill were reiterating previous comments that had been made about the bill. Time was running out, and I wanted them to experience a formal senate vote. I urged the senate to accept cloture, even though they had only 16, not 17, votes.

Legislative Action

In a loud determined voice, someone cried out "**Let's walk out. That way we won't have to vote on it.**" Students began to leave the room. Some stomped off alone, others left hesitantly with friends. They waited outside the doorway and gathered together in the hallway. They looked both bewildered and exhilarated. I was witnessing their first public act of civil disobedience.

Back in the room, there were 13 hopeful senators unified in a group ready to vote on the Clean Air Act. This group had just enough senators to form a quorum. The majority leader took over and called out the names of the senators. When their names were called, each announced his or her supporting vote for the bill. Midway through this process, however, one of the senators unexpectedly decided to leave. Her exit disrupted the voting process. The senate no longer had a quorum, and so the voting was suspended.

Class Meeting

In our debriefing about the experience, students had a variety of explanations for their actions. Those who opposed the Clean Air Act felt that if they remained in the senate for the vote, there was a chance that the legislation would pass. By engaging in a dramatic protest action, they calculated that it might attract the undecided to join them. In contrast, those who remained in the room were strongly in favor of the legislation.

This was an awakening experience for all. The class did not act as one in this event. There were multiple perspectives and interpretations. Some students admitted being influenced by the words and actions of their peers. Others revealed their commitments to their constituent bases and how this guided their respective positions on the bill. There were still others who revealed the difficulty of making decisions when they were not ready to take a stand. Sharing and listening to multiple perspectives about this situation helped students to realize that people encounter an experience in idiosyncratic ways.

Adding Additional Layers to the Legislative Process

Like an accordion in design, curriculum drama can adapt to limitless configurations. Here are some activities that you can do to add additional dimensions to the senate experience:

❑ Include a session where senators propose and vote upon amendments to the legislation. Resource M contains a sample amendment form.

❑ Create a media event so that senators have a public venue for promoting (or critiquing) legislation. This can take place in a newsmaker interview or in a panel discussion.

❑ Construct a letter from the U.S. president to the senators stating the president's position on a senate bill.

The classroom senate is about opening up new possibilities of being in the world. Within their community of legislative practice, students can develop a powerful sense of agency. As seen in these depictions of two senate debates, students invested in new topics of conversation and engaged in productive ways of taking public action within the classroom setting. Students had freedom of choice and freedom of movement. The Security and Immigration Committee decided against further action with S 121, "Reducing Crime," and the bill died in committee. In the second debate, the senators showed their position on S 125, "Clean Air," by either staying in or leaving the classroom. In these instances, student actions went far beyond simply committing to an answer on a multiple choice test.

Success hinged on the ability of a group to collaborate. Nowhere was this more apparent than in the final moments of the classroom senate. Opponents to the Clean Air Act took measures not as students resisting a teacher's authority, but rather as senators inflamed at the attempt to limit debate. They knew they had the freedom and the authority as senators to walk out of a senate proceeding.

Perhaps even more amazing was the other contingent of senators who remained in the classroom to vote for the Clean Air Act. They identified with and believed in the long term benefits of this bill.

The success of either group depended upon its ability to stay united. In the end, one contingent was more successful, and so the legislation did not pass. As their teacher, I applauded both groups' actions. It was evident that through their participation in the curriculum drama, students had developed a profound sense of engagement and agency in the classroom senate.

Summary

The classroom senate is a venue where students identify issues, appraise ideas, and address conflicts. They participate within a "community of practice" (Lave & Wenger, 1991). In so doing, students connect with others to generate complex understandings about the legislative branch of government.

Student energy powers the direction of curriculum drama. In this particular instance, students propose the legislation they want to initiate, they determine the meaning of political labels within their respective parties, they pose the questions they want to ask the witnesses in the senate hearing, and they decide to take public positions on prioritized legislation.

What's Next?

Chapter 9, "Constructing Curriculum Drama in Other Contexts," explores how this approach can be constructed in other areas of social studies. Three situations are briefly explored:

- Constructing a World Summit: Explore current events by constructing and participating in a world summit on peace.
- Constructing a Town Meeting: Examine women's suffrage by creating and engaging in a town hall meeting during the 1800s.
- Constructing a Criminal Trial: Investigate the judicial system by constructing and being part of a criminal trial.

9

Constructing Curriculum Drama in Other Contexts

Curriculum drama forms a bridge that links the tasks of teaching, learning, and inquiry to the authentic interests, concerns, and energies of students. In the case of the legislative drama as described in the previous chapters, students became absorbed in the world of legislation; they constructed and took action on bills that reflected their own preoccupations with the world around them. By investigating the legislative structures defined within Article 1 of the U.S. Constitution and examining the existing practices and traditions within today's U.S. Senate, we transformed the classroom and our interactions within it to a legislative experience.

Can curriculum drama work in other social studies contexts? This chapter showcases different ways to construct transformed worlds within the classroom. Rather than studying about a topic, students engage as inside players within a constructed context.

Current Events: World Summit on Peace

Civic Action: Students *as renowned peace activists* through time interact with one another at a world summit.

Setting the Stage

Whether it is from video games, lyrics from contemporary music, or movie or television programs, we are exposed to a steady diet of violence, human suffering, and tragedy. Rather than become overwhelmed by this grim reality, how can we take notice of the work that has been done in contemporary and in historical times to develop peace around the world? Based on the initiative and ideas of leaders of peace, how can we take action to develop and sustain peace in contemporary times?

Triggering Interest

The following lines of inquiry can be explored in class discussions, written reflections, or through encounters with art (e.g., visual art, music).

- What is peace? Is it simply the absence of war? Or is it something more (e.g., human rights, social justice, nonviolence)?
- What are symbols of peace?
- What does peace look like? Sound like? Feel like?
- What are different ways to build peace?
- Does peace mean the same thing to different people?
- Where do people engage in the work for international peace (e.g., the Peace Palace at The Hague, United Nations, nongovernment organizations)?
- What has been written on peace (e.g., poetry, speeches, lyrics, essays)?

A Gallery Walk: Making Peace Visible

Locate diverse images and symbols of peace and post these images at eye level in the classroom or in the hallway. Make time for students to take a "gallery walk" to deeply observe these images. What patterns do they notice about these images? What image is most memorable?

Encourage students to locate additional visuals around the theme of peace. In this way the gallery can be continually updated. Have students engage in a variety of peace-related, open-ended activities. Working in pairs, they can

❑ pose questions or comments about various images; these can then be posted alongside the image.

> ❑ list the sounds they hear in an image.
> ❑ title the images—students can then provide a spoken (or written) rationale for their title.
> ❑ bring in (or compose) music that can accompany a particular image.

Enticement: An Invitation to a World Summit

Invite students to attend a "world summit" on peace. What events happen in a world summit? Brainstorm with students about the speakers they wish to hear at this event. These individuals can be anyone from local community helpers (e.g., fire chief) to renowned figures (e.g., the Dalai Lama, Mother Theresa). They can come from long ago (e.g., Frederick Douglass, Jane Addams) to current times (e.g., current Nobel Peace Prize recipients). They can be political leaders (e.g., Gandhi, Martin Luther King, Jr.), architects who have designed contemplative spaces (e.g., Maya Lin), or consumer protection advocates (e.g., Ralph Nader). Consider also artists who have advanced the cause for peace through their work (e.g., musicians, poets, visual artists).

Tool of Practice: Constructing a Dossier

Have each student construct a dossier on a peace activist who plans to attend this summit. This set of documents will contain background information (e.g., date of birth, country of origin), timeline of pivotal events in the activist's life, and when possible actual texts of published speeches from this individual. Once dossiers are complete, the class as a whole can engage in a number of inquiries:

- Which of our leaders of peace is the oldest? Youngest?
- Which ones lived during the same time period?
- Which of our guests has the longest trip to make through time? Through geographic distance?

Letter of Invitation

After studying about their designated leaders of peace, students can then write a formal letter to this individual to invite him or her to the world summit on peace. This letter can include a section where the writer highlights the leader's contributions to peace. Students can then "mail" these letters in the classroom "mailbox." As a class, decide whether it makes sense to use two mailboxes—one for delivery to the world of the living and the other for delivery to the world of the past.

Another Idea: Submitting a Conference Proposal

Students as leaders of peace can first submit conference proposals to this upcoming summit. This can be a 50 word abstract of what they are intending to present. Many conferences offer a variety of presentation formats: formal talk, panel discussion, small group sessions, poster exhibit. In their proposal, students can indicate the format that best describes how they plan to present the work of their chosen figures.

Once students have received formal acceptance from the "conference organizers," they can begin to prepare their presentations for the conference.

From Studying About to Portraying

Have students examine the dossiers they constructed about their leaders. What are notable words, repeated phrases, and key ideas from these documents? Have the class explore how best to portray their respective peace activists in a way that makes sense to each student.

Welcome to the World Summit!

The following ideas are designed to help spur belief in the transformed world of the classroom setting.

- "Checking in" at the registration desk (outside the classroom), can serve as a preliminary cue for students about the classroom transformation to a world summit. Upon their on-site registration for this event, participants can then pick up their conference folders containing their official name tags, desk cards, and programs as well as loose leaf paper and a pencil.
- Members of the hospitality committee can welcome each guest to the conference (e.g., "We are honored that you could come;" "We are so looking forward to your talk"). Double check the conference list to make sure that each leader's name (not the student's name) is properly registered. The hospitality crew can pose questions to each participant to further the sense

that they are entering a new world (e.g., "Is this your first time here?" "How was your flight?"). Students can play roles as both peace leaders *and* as official helpers (e.g., members of the hospitality committee.)

Multiple Entry Points

What are the different ways that students can engage in this world peace summit? The following ideas are meant to entice students to take ownership of their positions within the experience.

Student Choice

Faced with the task of having to publicly speak the words and ideas of their chosen leader, students can select from a variety of options:

- Speech (as a keynote speaker or one of the featured speakers)
- Talking points (informal sharing in a small group setting)
- Poster session (showing visually this person's contribution to peace)

In whatever format they select, students will not be talking *about* their featured leader of peace. Instead they will portray or embody that individual's ideas and contributions toward peace based on their own research efforts and in a way that seems credible.

Participating in a Task Force

Along with working to become a chosen leader of peace, students could also participate in an administrative committee or task force. Students will certainly have their own suggestions about what needs to be done for this big event; here are a few ideas to get started:

- Community building

Peace gatherings inevitably include a way to create a sense of community. Members of this committee are charged with the task of planning an event that will bring people together.

Ideas: Informal meal

Sing-a-long

Film and discussion

Viewing flowers in a nearby garden

- Hospitality

People come from a distance to attend world summits. Members of this committee are charged with the task of making visitors, speakers, and observers feel welcomed.

Ideas: Create name and desk cards for speakers and conference participants.

Design program cover for all visitors.

Welcome people when they arrive at the summit.

Make peace banners for the event.

- Public relations

World summits are important events designed to heighten awareness and understanding. Members in this committee are charged with spreading the word about this event.

Ideas: Create a press release (e.g., for school paper, parent newsletter).

Construct a guest list (e.g., for parents, staff, and administrators).

- Next steps

Taking action is a key element in peace conferences. Members of this committee are charged with the task of recommending a plan of action that summit members will take to ensure that the march toward peace continues to grow and be strong.

Alternative Ideas: Exploring Movements and Organizations

Rather than looking at individuals, the class may wish to investigate historical movements, organizations, or religions that seek to make the world a better place. Students can invite representatives from among the following:

❑ Movements
  ○ Abolition of slavery
  ○ Civil rights
  ○ Women's rights
❑ Organizations
  ○ Doctors Without Borders, http://www.doctorswithoutborders.org
  ○ Habitat for Humanity International, http://www.habitat.org

○ Humane Society, http://www.hsus.org
○ Women's International League for Peace and Freedom, http://www.wilpf.org
○ NAACP, http://www.naacp.org
❏ Belief systems
  ○ Atheism
  ○ Buddhism
  ○ Christianity
  ○ Hinduism
  ○ Islam
  ○ Judaism
  ○ Shintoism

Using Blueprints

In the world summit, students will use their research and the materials included in their constructed dossier as a blueprint for forming a frame of reference around their chosen peace activist. As they portray their leaders and the leaders' accomplishments in the field of peace, encourage students to weave excerpts from the leaders' work (e.g., written ideas, speeches) in casual conversations, formal speeches, and group discussions.

Along with individual dossiers, this curriculum drama also uses another blueprint—the format of a world summit. How are official and nongovernmental world summits structured? Through investigations, the class can construct their own format for this experience.

Structuring the World Summit

Using the general blueprint of conferences, you and your students can decide upon an event, or a sequence of events, for a world summit. Here are some ideas to get started:

1. Opening ceremony
  Community-building event

2. Plenary session
  Welcoming remarks
  Keynote speaker
  Featured speakers

(Continued)

(Continued)

3. Break-out sessions/poster sessions
   In small groups, each leader of peace could share a significant moment in her or his life's work. Those who constructed posters can portray their vision and impact. Each group can then discuss ways for making the current world a better, more peaceful place. Time permitting, leaders within this setting can construct a resolution for ideas on how to sustain and develop world peace.

4. Plenary session
   Sharing and voting on resolutions
   Keynote speaker
   Sample title for speech: "Next Steps: Taking Action for Peace"
   Concluding remarks

5. Closing ceremony
   Community-building event

The summit can be as simple or as lavish as the teacher and the class decide. The key point to this work however, is that students are working alongside the teacher to coconstruct this experience. In this way the curriculum drama reflects student-teacher choices, student interests, and student research. Students are likely to be receptive to and enthused about this event when they have been an integral part of its construction process.

1. Opening Ceremony

To signal the opening of this summit, the world leaders might want to engage in a preliminary experience that will help them to focus their energies on the theme of peace. For instance, they could engage in a sustained moment of collective silence or listen to the sound of peace (e.g., ringing of a chime).

2. Plenary Session 1

After the opening ceremony, the plenary session could begin with welcoming comments to all. Participants can briefly introduce the leaders of peace who are seated next to them. The keynote and featured speakers can then deliver their talks. To heighten both the formality and the break from the ordinary, a podium (or music stand) can be used by the keynote and featured speakers. Time permitting, there can be a question and answer session so as to engage the audience directly with the featured speakers.

3. Break-out Session/Poster Sessions

Using their well-researched talking points, world leaders in this session could discuss their lives and the contributions they are making (or have made) toward peace. As a collaborative task, members of each group can then use their selected characters' unique vantage points to discuss strategies for making the contemporary world a more peaceful place. Time permitting, each group can construct a written resolution on this matter.

To ensure that these small group sessions are productive, you or your program committee may want to decide how these groups should be organized. Should people who lived in the same time period be placed at the same table? Or should people who worked on similar causes be seated together? What if people who were from the same geographic region were clustered together? These are decisions that students can help make.

4. Plenary Session 2

When they return to the plenary session, members of each group could present their resolutions to the entire summit. If there is time in the schedule, a special committee can be formed to construct one cohesive document from these group resolutions. This document can then be shared, discussed, and voted upon by all the participants on the last day of the conference. If time permits, participants can offer amendments to this world resolution.

The plenary session could conclude with a final keynote speaker and concluding remarks from the chief organizer of the event. This would be an opportune time to thank both the leaders of peace for coming and the students of peace for preparing and hosting such a wonderful event.

5. Closing Ceremony

There are a number of ways to conclude the world summit experience. Working with members of your program committee or the class as a whole, decide on a mutually acceptable format.

For instance, you might want to consider a peace march! As a culminating experience, world summit participants could walk through the school hallways or around the school's neighborhood as a way to draw attention to the cause for peace.

Constructing a Peace March

In designing a peace march, the class (or program committee) needs to decide how it should be structured. These questions are meant to get ideas flowing:

- Should participants march quickly or slowly? In pairs or singularly?
- Should the participants be silent? Laughing? Singing?
- Should the march itself be led by the slow beating of a drum? Playing of a flute? Ringing of chimes?
- Should placards be created and used in this march? If so, what messages should be included?
- Who should lead this march?
- For points of comparison, students could investigate the tactics used in marches from the past (e.g., those of civil right activists or suffragists).

From beginning to end, the transformed world of the classroom challenges students in multiple ways. Not only are they faced with the task of portraying in a credible way a renowned leader of peace, but they are also interacting with peers who have studied and who are also portraying in their own unique ways the perspectives of various peace activists. Through the process of setting the stage, constructing the event based on credible blueprints and devising entry points for participation, students can build sustained belief in this classroom experience. By so doing, they can develop complex understandings about the concept of peace and the individuals who have made a substantive mark in this field.

History: Should Women Vote?

Civic Action: Students *as participants in a town hall meeting* during the nineteenth century, discuss whether women should have the right to vote.

Setting the Stage

March has been designated women's history month, and yet it can be difficult for students to truly understand and appreciate the societal challenges that women in this nation have faced in their quest to obtain one of the most basic rights as citizens—the right to vote. This curriculum drama engages the class to embody various positions on this once controversial issue.

Triggering Interest

Involve students in the task of setting policy on various topics pertinent to the classroom. By working in small groups, students could write down their recommendations. Here are some ideas:

Social dynamics: What recommendations do you have for making sure that people feel included and not isolated in this classroom?

Homework: What makes for an intriguing homework assignment or project?

Arrival/Dismissal: What ideas do you have for making classroom transitions more orderly?

Assessment: What makes for a fair test? A fair quiz?

Community work: What ideas do you have for designing a community based project with a younger grade in your school?

After each topic has been discussed in a small group and amended and voted upon by the entire class, inform the class that as the teacher you will take their recommendations under advisement and will let them know at a future time about your executive decision.

In a written reflection or as a full class discussion, encourage students to explore this activity and their role within it. How did it feel to participate in the building of class policy? How did it feel to vote on these issues as a class? To what extent did people feel empowered?

Now lead the class in a discussion about how it would be if only some were allowed to participate and not others.

Enticement: Taking a Trip . . . to the Nineteenth Century

Invite students to a town hall meeting back in time (early part of the nineteenth century) where the topic has been raised in a small community about whether it makes sense for women to have the right to vote.

Multiple Blueprints

The Library of Congress is a treasure trove for social studies teachers interested in using primary documents within their classrooms. To access material related to U.S. history and culture, use the library's American Memory link (http://memory.loc.gov). You will find a vast collection of easily accessible material categorized under more than 100 topics. Once at this site, click on "Women's History" and locate the link "Votes for Women: Selections from the National American Woman Suffrage Association Collection, 1848–1921" where you can access a wide range of historical resources (e.g., news articles, speeches, court testimony). For example, Resource N contains excerpts from a debaters' handbook published in 1910 (Phelps, 1910) that outlines the key arguments in support of and in opposition to women's suffrage.

As a class, brainstorm the type of people who might be interested in attending this town hall meeting. For example, some might be

- people wanting to uphold societal traditions.
- people seeking to change the status quo.
- people wanting to be more informed about the issues.
- community leaders (e.g., clergy, mayor, teacher).
- news reporters from various publications.

Field Trip: Town Hall Meeting

If possible, schedule a class trip to a town hall meeting (or a council meeting). Have students take note of what happens at this event. If these meetings are scheduled after school hours, could parents or caregivers take their children? Another idea is to have the class interview adults (e.g., parents, community leaders) who have attended these events. What makes for a successful town hall meeting?

Have students read aloud and discuss various documents on women's suffrage. Here are excerpts from two such documents, *Solitude of Self* by Elizabeth Cady Stanton and *The True Woman: A Series of Discourses* by Rev. J. D. Fulton, as well as some section titles from a third.

Elizabeth Cady Stanton, Solitude of Self

Committee of the Judiciary
U.S. Congress
1892

In discussing the rights of woman, we are to consider, first, what belongs to her as an individual, in a world of her own. . . . Her rights under such circumstances are to use all her faculties for her own safety and happiness.

Secondly, if we consider her as a citizen, as a member of a great nation, she must have the same rights as all other members, according to the fundamental principles of our Government.

Thirdly, viewed as a woman, an equal factor in civilization, her rights and duties are still the same—individual happiness and development. . . .

SOURCE: Stanton (1915).

With Internet access to the Library of Congress, students can access *The Blue Book* (Björkman & Porritt, 1917), which countered anti-suffrage arguments. Sections had such titles as the following:

- The ignorant wife
- The bad women's vote
- Cease to be respected
- Too emotional

Rev. J. D. Fulton, *Woman Versus Ballot*

Tremont Temple, Boston
1869

Three facts stand in the way of Woman's being helped by the Ballot,—God, Nature and Common Sense. . . .

It is patent to everyone that this attempt to secure the ballot for woman is a revolt against the position and sphere assigned to woman by God himself. . . .

It is because the ballot has a tendency to make woman the rival rather than the companion of man, that it is opposed to the purest sentiments of woman. She wishes no division, and cannot tolerate independence or separation from the object of her love. . . .

SOURCE: Fulton (1869).

From the National American Woman Suffrage Association, Collection, 1848–1921, (http://memory.loc.gov), search for the link

"Selected Articles on Women Suffrage." This will lead you to other antisuffrage documents, such as the following:

- *Problem of Woman Suffrage*
- *Why the Home Makers Do Not Want to Vote*
- *Facts and Fallacies About Woman Suffrage*
- *Negative Discussion: Some Facts About Suffrage and Anti Suffrage* by Gilbert Jones

Logistics

Once students have explored and discussed various writings on this topic, have students decide on the positions and characters they want to construct for this event. If the aim of your lesson is to show the force of majority opinion in its opposition to woman's suffrage, then limit the number of students who will voice support for the right to vote. If the aim of your lesson is to show how a community was divided over this issue, then provide for a more even distribution of those who will construct arguments in favor of and in opposition to women's suffrage. (Remember also to include those who may be undecided.)

Along with local members of the community, your town meeting might also include a surprise visit from a renowned public speaker who had a position on this issue. Here are some ideas:

- Susan B. Anthony
- Frederick Douglass
- William Lloyd Garrison
- Francis Watkins Harper
- Lucretia Mott
- Elizabeth Cady Stanton
- Sojourner Truth

Who Plays Which Role?

Work with the class to determine the system for constructing positions to portray. Here are three options:

Lottery: Each student picks a number from a hat. The student who obtains the number ı makes the first choice in deciding which role to portray.

Negotiated:	Students write down their idea of who they would like to be at this town hall meeting and the position they would like to take on women's suffrage. The teacher works with the class to make final determinations.
Random:	Determine beforehand the number of people who will portray prosuffrage, antisuffrage, and undecided positions in the town hall meeting. Mark these positions on pieces of paper and have students draw pieces of paper from a hat indicating defined perspectives.

Time to Construct Positions

Once students are clear about the positions they are going to construct, have them work with like-minded people so as to build their arguments and to locate primary documents that support their positions. Have them highlight notable quotes from these texts, so that the quotes are readily available for the students' use at the town hall meeting. Along these lines, students might want to prepare talking points to help them organize their thoughts.

Constructing the Environment

Decide with the students how to arrange the class environment for a town meeting. There are many options. You can arrange an intimate setting, where chairs are arranged in a circle. Or it can be a more formal setup, where the town leader sits behind a front table and the citizens of the town sit in rows, facing a speaker's podium.

Thinking Ahead

What should be the guidelines for participating in a town meeting? This is a topic that you and your class will need to decide. Should people stand when they are given permission to speak? May the audience readily respond to speaker comments? Should the town meeting break for an intermission so that people can informally talk with one another about the topic under discussion?

Multiple Entry Points

On the day of the scheduled event, how can we trigger entry into a different time and place? This can happen in many ways. Sometimes introductory comments can serve as the necessary springboard to a transformed world. Sometimes a different room arrangement or ritual can help students in their imaginary leap to this new setting and era. For others, the entry point may not happen until dramatic tension surfaces from events that emerge from this town hall meeting.

Welcoming Remarks

Introductory remarks and rituals can provide a collective entry point for involvement in the transformed world within the classroom. Arrange for a student to lead this session. Here is an example of how introductory remarks and a patriotic ritual provided an entry point into this curriculum drama:

> Thank you all for coming to this Town Hall meeting on this blustery, winter's evening. Let's first rise and pledge allegiance to our flag.
>
> Our new wood stove (nodding to an imaginary place in the classroom) is working hard to provide us with needed warmth.
>
> As a community, we also need to work hard to continue to be good neighbors.
>
> It has come to the attention of the town leaders, however, that there appears to be a serious division between us, and I am worried that our lovely community might be in peril. I understand that neighbors are not talking to one another because of different views on this contemporary topic—women's suffrage.
>
> For this reason, the town leaders have arranged for our community to meet and discuss the question, "Should women have the right to vote?" As a community, let's share our thoughts about this topic in an informed and respectful manner.

Admittedly, it can be daunting to coconstruct an event with the class without knowing how it is going to turn out. It is certainly more unpredictable than a scripted lesson in a textbook. At the same time, however, know that students' participation in this experience will be based in part on their readings of the historical record. Their public statements at this town meeting will include text from primary documents and quotes from historical figures. In addition, this experience will provide insight into how people of the past thought about the role of women in society. Furthermore, students will not be studying *about* history; they will be engaged *within* the field itself.

Law: A Criminal Trial

Civic Action: Students *as members of the criminal justice system* (e.g., jury, witnesses, attorneys, judge) critically explore the criminal actions and motivations of an individual encountered in a work of fiction (or from the historical record).

Setting the Stage

The criminal justice system provides a ready context for curriculum drama. In this instance, the class transforms an episode that occurred in a work of fiction (e.g., murder, defacement of property, theft) to critical scrutiny within a court of law. What were the mitigating circumstances surrounding this crime? Who could testify on behalf of the defendant? On behalf of the prosecution?

Another Idea

Rather than staging a criminal trial based on the actions of a character in a novel, consider the idea of bringing charges against a historical figure.

Accused: Christopher Columbus

Charges: murder, slavery, theft

Defense witnesses: Queen Isabella and King Ferdinand, crew members

Prosecution witnesses: Bartolomé de Las Casas (witnessed devastation in Hispaniola), Taino people

The works of Howard Zinn (Zinn, 2003; Zinn & Arnov, 2004) provide both historical background and primary documents for pivotal events within U.S. history. Well referenced and accessible, they are valuable texts for the critically informed social studies educator.

Triggering Interest

What do students know about law? Have any been to an actual courtroom? Would it be possible to arrange a field trip to a courtroom? Are all courtrooms the same? What patterns, if any, do they notice about these rooms?

Could a criminal lawyer visit the classroom and discuss the intricacies of the judicial system? Before the attorney's visit, have students construct a list of questions that they could ask. Consider the following:

- What makes for a strong witness?
- What qualities does a lawyer look for in a potential juror, and how does one identify these qualities in a juror?
- Does the jury always make the right decision?

No Time for a Trial? Enact a Grand Jury Investigation

If your schedule does not permit a full trial, construct instead a grand jury investigation. This occurs before a trial. The jury hears the evidence and determines whether or not to *indict*, or formally charge, the defendant. If the majority of the jury feels there is insufficient evidence, then the suspect is not charged with a crime. If, on the other hand, the jury feels there is "probable cause," then the suspect is indicted with the crime, and a trial date is set.

The text *Rethinking Columbus* (Bigelow, 1998) has ideas for bringing multiple indictments against various parties connected to the devastation of the people of Hispaniola in the years after 1492.

Enticement: Determining the Criminal Charge

Invite students to participate in a criminal justice system by examining the crime(s) that took place in a novel (or a historical event). If multiple crimes took place, determine as a class which criminal action should be the focus and which individual should be indicted or formally charged.

Along with the list of characters who are somewhat connected to the defendant, brainstorm a list of the people who work in a courtroom (e.g., judge, attorneys, bailiff, jury, court reporter). Combine these lists, and have students determine who gets to play which role in the criminal case.

Work to support a wide variety of students in taking on high-profile roles. In your position as the supportive teacher, engage in private conversations with the more introverted individuals to gently encourage them to consider taking on leadership positions. High-profile roles (e.g., attorneys) should not be limited to those individuals who are at ease with thinking, speaking, or participating in the public domain. This is the time when all students should have the opportunity to stretch themselves and to experience new leadership positions.

An Idea: Team Approach

It can be daunting for a single attorney to have the fate of the defendant on his or her shoulders! For this reason, I advocate that students work in teams to fill high-profile positions, such as those of judge or attorney. There could be two or three justices, a team of defense attorneys, and a team of prosecuting attorneys. Teams of students can even play pivotal witnesses. This removes the onus on the individual, and it can build collaborative work skills within each team.

Multiple Blueprints

Before the actual trial, students could construct witness statements based on their characters' perspectives. If the novel or story from which the characters are drawn include actual quotes, then the students as characters can use those quotes in their witness statements or when they are on the witness stand. In this way, the novel serves as a loose blueprint for developing the characters. For those who are developing their characters based on courtroom responsibilities (e.g., bailiff, attorneys, justices), the practice of law can serve as a guide.

Another blueprint is courtroom protocols and procedures. It helps for the students to know beforehand that the two teams of lawyers address their comments directly to the judge—not to each other. In addition, remind the class that the witness is expected to respond to the questions posed by the attorneys. In the event that the witness does not know the answer or cannot remember a particular detail, then she or he may state "I don't know" or "I don't recall."

Based on time constraints, it might be necessary to adjust criminal procedure within the classroom. The trial can take place in one session or over the course of several days. I use the following format in my classroom:

1. Bailiff's Announcement

Bailiff announces "All rise, the honorable Justices [names of justices] are presiding in the case People of [name of state] versus [name of defendant]." (*Once announced, the judges walk in, and all stand until the judges sit down.*)

2. Opening Statements: Framing the Trial

Judges request the prosecution team to provide an opening statement, and this is followed by the defense team's opening statement.

3. Testimony

The prosecution team calls the first witness. The bailiff swears in the witness: "Do you agree to tell the truth, the whole truth, and nothing but the truth?" In a direct examination, the prosecution elicits testimony from this individual. The defense then cross-examines this witness.

The defense teams calls their first witness. The bailiff swears in the witness. The defense elicits testimony from this individual. The prosecution then cross-examines this witness.

Depending upon the time available, the attorneys could take turns calling on various witnesses.

4. Closing Statement: Framing the Trial

Upon determining that all pertinent witnesses have provided testimony, the judges request the prosecution team to provide a closing statement, followed by the defense team's closing statement.

5. Instructions to the Jury

The judges provide guidelines to the jury about the meaning of the charges brought against the defendant and instruct the jury about the deliberation process.

6. Jury Deliberation

Before the jury is sent into a separate room, they will decide upon a foreperson. Once a decision is made by the jury, the court reconvenes, and the foreperson reads the verdict aloud.

Points of Comparison

In a constructed trial, there will inevitably be a need to adapt procedures to the classroom setting. For instance, in a criminal courtroom, the jury first hears all the witnesses for the prosecution, then the witnesses for the defense. In the classroom courtroom, the prosecution and the defense take turns calling their respective witnesses.

During our debriefing about the classroom experience, I draw attention to how we deviate from legal procedure. This then provides an accessible and memorable way to teach about the criminal justice system. It is first grounded in hands-on classroom experience and then used as a point of comparison to understand the judicial process within society.

Once the trial is in motion, the students will go well beyond the initial blueprints of their constructed characters. In the course of embodying their characters, students may provide detail in their testimony that is not actually written in the novel. Nonetheless, students in this context can develop a deeper appreciation of the novel as they work to bring their characters to life; at the same time, they are engaged in the intricacies of the criminal justice system.

Multiple Entry Points

A classroom trial can be a galvanizing experience. Whether a student is a member of the jury, an attorney, a judge, the bailiff, or a potential witness, the courtroom setting provides for unpredictable drama and suspense. Regardless of the role that each student plays, everyone becomes at some point an active participant in the courtroom.

> **Putting History on Trial**
>
> If instead of a character in a novel, you are using an actual individual from history, students can use primary documents from that designated time period as their blueprints for constructing their characters.

Triggering a Buzz of Anticipation

In the days preceding the trial, I post signs inside and outside the classroom alerting the school community about the event. For instance, after the class read Steinbeck's *Of Mice and Men*, we held a trial in which the state of California tried George Milton in the murder of Lennie Small. Even though we were not actually in California, we pretended that we were in a courtroom there. I posted the sign shown here.

In addition, I construct a sign indicating who has which position as witnesses, attorneys, and bailiff. Everything is transparent in this sit-

> **Criminal Trial**
>
> *State of California v. George Milton*
> *February 27, 2009*
> Charge: Murder in the first degree
> Honorable Justice [last name of student] presiding.

uation. Sometimes we include the role of court reporter, who is in charge of tape recording the proceedings, and a sketch artist, who is in charge of doing quick illustrations of pivotal moments in the trial. As is shown in the box below, no one is restricted by gender to play a particular character.

Defense attorneys:	Mr. Blitz and Ms. Turk
Prosecuting attorneys:	Ms. Provia and Mr. Wright
Court bailiff:	Ms. Viera
Arresting officer:	Ms. Thaw
George Milton:	Ms. Mill
Lennie Small (deceased):	Mr. Law
Candy:	Ms. Cape
Curley:	Mr. Straus
Crooks:	Ms. Mix
Slim:	Ms. Glick
Curley's wife (deceased):	Mr. Shin

Depending upon the decision of the class, we sometimes stretch our imaginations and invite the deceased to testify at the trial! For instance, in George Milton's trial, we listened to the testimony of Curley's wife and Lennie Small.

The only names I do not post are of those who are serving on the jury. Even though everyone in this situation knows who they are, as they are classmates, I make a point of not posting their names. This then triggers a discussion about why it is important to protect the privacy of jurors.

Interviewing the Witnesses

Have the class determine those witnesses who might offer testimony that supports the defendant's case and those who might support the prosecution's case. In the days before the trial, have both the prosecution and defense teams interview their respective witnesses to ensure that everyone is clear about the details of the case.

Changing the Room Arrangement

If it is at all possible, reconfigure the classroom to a courtroom setting. Place the judges in a prominent and central location and the prosecution and defense in separate areas of the room. There should be a witness stand, adjacent to the judge's desk. Nearby there should be a row of chairs for the jury.

On the day of the trial, all students could receive desk cards that indicate their constructed roles; I make these desk cards by folding an eight-by-five index card in half and writing the character's name in magic marker on the blank side. When a witness comes to testify, the bailiff brings out the appropriate desk card and places it on the witness stand.

Ownership

Have each witness construct a statement ahead of time that introduces the character and his or her perspective. The witness can read this preliminary statement when asked "Please state your name, occupation, and relationship to the defendant."

Judicial Terminology

Attorneys might raise objections about a particular question posed to a witness (e.g., leading the witness, hearsay, not qualified to answer). The judge can respond in two ways:

Sustained:	This means that the judge has ruled that the original question needs to be rephrased or withdrawn.
Overruled:	This means that the judge has ruled that the question is permitted.

At any point, the judge(s) might request the attorneys to "approach the bench" for a private conversation.

As the teacher, I try to stay on the sidelines, and I work at being the impartial but helpful on-site legal advisor to all parties in the courtroom. From time to time, the judges might consult with me about an attorney's objection. Sometimes I might whisper to some attorneys about a particular question they might want to pose to a witness or an objection that they might want to raise. For the most part, however, I try not to impede the pursuit of justice in our curriculum drama.

Using Stories to Construct a Criminal Trial

Here are ideas for bringing criminal charges to some notable characters.

Defendant	Story	Criminal Charges
Younger grades		
Goldilocks	*Goldilocks and the Three Bears*	trespass/property damage
Wolf	*Three Little Pigs*	property damage
Hansel	*Hansel and Gretel*	trespass
Older grades		
Achilles	*The Iliad*	murder
Odysseus	*The Odyssey*	murder

In a criminal trial, the class goes way beyond being conversant about a literary plot (or a historical event). Instead, they become deeply involved in filling in the blanks and adding dimension to a particular character (or historical figure). At the same time, they develop experience as insiders in the criminal justice system.

Concluding Words: Letting the World In

Curriculum as curriculum drama seeks to let the world into the classroom—with all its messiness, all its contradictions, and all its complications. This approach puts into motion what there is to know about a given topic and entices the participating individuals to know more, so that they can engage more skillfully with their peers and contribute in more strategic ways within the transformed setting. At the same time, because the class is interacting within this new setting, there is considerable recognition and value placed on informed understandings within peer interactions. Driven by primary documents, current practices, or events within the field of study, curriculum drama builds upon relevant concepts and content understandings.

Curriculum drama triggers a dynamic interplay between imagination and inquiry, content and pedagogy, knowing and questioning. It is my hope that educators will be inspired to collaborate with their students to construct curriculum dramas of their own. For I believe that classrooms are places where we critically "read the world" (Freire, 1996) and where we become "provoked to come awake and find new visions, new ways of living in the fragile human world" (Greene, 2001, p. 207).

Resource A—Oath of Office

Since 1862, U.S. senators publicly state *and* in writing confirm an oath of office. For more information, go to http://www.senate.gov.

Senator's Oath of Office

I do solemnly swear (or affirm) that I will support and defend the Constitution of the United States against all enemies, foreign and domestic; that I will bear true faith and allegiance to the same; that I take this obligation freely, without any mental reservation or purpose of evasion; and that I will well and faithfully discharge the duties of the office on which I am about to enter: So help me God.

Senator _____

　　　　　(first name)　　　　　　　　　　　　　　　　　　　　　　　　　(last name)

Senator's signature _____

Place where oath was taken _____

　　　　　　　　　　　　(city/town)　　　　　　　　　　　　　　　　　　(state)

Date of oath _____

Resource B–Research Guidelines: State Report

Directions: As a senator, you want to know as much as you possibly can about your state and your constituents. This project is designed to help you deeply understand your state in a variety of different ways.

> **Cover:** Construct an artistic representation of your state. Ideas: state flag, motto, geographic outline of state
>
> **Text:** In a two- to three-page, typed paper, explore the geography, people and issues within your state. Each section should contain between two to three paragraphs.

Geography:
Two or three paragraphs

What are the geographic regions within your state? What are natural landmarks (e.g., river, canyon) within your state? Does the geography serve as a natural state border? What is the year-round climate? Do different regions of the state have different climate zones?

People:
Two or three paragraphs

What is the cultural background of the people who live in your state? What are the population trends within your state—are there more people now than ten years ago? What sort of occupations do people have? What are the high school graduation rates; how does this compare to the national average? How many people in your state are incarcerated; how does this compare to the national average?

Issues:
Two or three paragraphs

What are the current issues facing your state? Consider such topics as immigration, homelessness, drought, unemployment, and environment.

Web Resources:

These Web sites will help you in your work.

http://www.state.gov	Instead of writing "state," type in the two-letter state abbreviation (e.g., for New Jersey, type "http://www.nj.gov")
http://newslink.org/	newspapers around the country
http://www.senate.gov	link to U.S. senators
http://www.50states.com	basic information about each state

Texts:

Barone, M., & Cohen, R., *The Almanac of American Politics.* Washington, DC: National Journal Group.

Kashner, Z. (Ed.), *The World Almanac and Book of Facts.* New York: World Almanac Books.

Differentiation:

Needing an extra challenge?

- Explore the historical background of this state.
- Redesign the state's flag.
- Include the artistic achievements of an individual from this state (music, dance, drama, visual arts).

Needing a different structure?

Instead of writing your information in paragraph form, consider creating

- graphic organizers.
- talking points (10 essential facts for each category).
- a radio broadcast promoting your state.

Resource C—Research Guidelines: Getting to Know a U.S. Senator

Your name _____

Your state in the classroom senate _____

Directions: Complete the following chart for each of your U.S. senators. Then compare your data with those of your classmates.

Useful Web sites: http://bioguide.congress.gov, http://www.senate.gov

Name of U.S. senator	
Date of birth	
Home	
Education—Name of college	
Committees—list three	
Military service?	
Previous jobs	
Political party	
Your choice—What other information did you find about your U.S. senator?	

Resource D—Activity: Determining Political Affiliations

In the U.S. Congress, members of the House of Representatives and the Senate belong to political parties. Currently, there are two major parties—the Democrats and the Republicans.

Unlike the U.S. Congress, where legislators decide which party they want to belong to, in our senate you are placed in a particular group! Working with the other senators who are also in this same group, you will collectively determine your party's political direction and agenda. If you so decide, you can be the *new Democrats* or the *new Republicans.*

Directions: The chart below lists the states within our classroom senate. To preview the *potential* membership of Republican and Democratic groups within our senate, complete this assignment.

Task: Go to http://www.senate.gov

If a state has two U.S. senators who are Democrats, place two checks in the Democrat Group column in the table below. In our classroom senate, this senator will *most likely* be in the Democratic group.

If a state has two U.S. senators who are Republicans, place two checks in the Republican Group column. In our classroom senate, this senator will *most likely* be in the Republican group.

If a state has a U.S. senator in each of the two different parties, place one check on the Republican side and one check on the Democratic side. In our classroom senate, this senator will be placed with *either* the Democrats *or* the Republicans.

	Republican Group	Democratic Group
Alaska		
Arizona		
California		
Colorado		
Florida		

(partial listing of states within a classroom senate)

Resource E—List of Senators in a Classroom Senate*

Classroom Senate

Republicans

Sen. Leah Brown	Alaska
Sen. Jim Cape	Colorado
Sen. Amanda East	Oklahoma
Sen. Eli Helm	Utah
Sen. Chris King	North Carolina
Sen. Alex Koch	Florida
Sen. Abigail Law	Tennessee
Sen. Emma Provia	Arizona
Sen. Jorge Santos	Kansas
Sen. Lee Shin	Pennsylvania
Sen. Stan Straus	Montana
Sen. Vivian Thom	Texas
Sen. Vicky Viera	Indiana

Democrats

Sen. Bill Belt	Georgia
Sen. Mike Block	Michigan
Sen. Jill Fox	North Dakota
Sen. Diane Glick	Hawaii
Sen. Brian Kalim	New York
Sen. Pat Krip	California
Sen. Mary Mill	Massachusetts
Sen. Katie Mix	Louisiana
Sen. Jesse Small	New Jersey
Sen. Ellen Turk	New Mexico
Sen. Sue Vork	Illinois
Sen.Tom Wright	Washington

* All names listed here are pseudonyms.

Resource F—Activity: Working on a Political Platform

Directions:

Working in your political party, identify four to six issues of major concern. For each issue write a paragraph outlining your party's position on this topic. Write broadly, not in detail; the specifics will come from legislation.

Resources:

As the new Democrats and the new Republicans, you are free to select issues that are meaningful to you. To obtain ideas, talk with each other and explore the Web sites of both parties:

U.S. Senate Democrats: http://democrats.senate.gov

U.S. Senate Republicans: http://republican.senate.gov

An Idea:

Once you have identified four to six issues, create smaller committees within your group, so that each team can focus on one issue. Each team will then be responsible for drafting a statement of their issue and position for inclusion in the platform statement.

CONSTRUCTING A POLITICAL PLATFORM

_____

(Name of political group)

Senators   _____   _____

              _____   _____

Introductory Statement:

What is your group's vision for the United States? What issues does your group intend to address during this senate experience?

Issue Number 1 _____

_____

Issue Number 2 _____

_____

_____

Resource G—Activity: Creating Legislation

S _____
(Senate number will be assigned)

In the classroom senate

_____
(date)

Sen. _____ introduced the following bill:

_____
(name of bill)

Purpose: _____

_____

Provisions:

1. _____

_____

_____

2. _____

_____

_____

Resource H—Committee Tasks

Task Number 1: Become familiar with all bills in your committee.

Have all individuals read or summarize their legislation.

Have the committee respond by posing questions or comments.

Have each committee elect a chairperson.

Task Number 2: Prioritize the committee's bills.

As a committee, decide which legislation addresses the most urgent national issue.

Is there a way to include aspects of the other bills into this prioritized legislation?

Task Number 3: Become knowledgeable about the bill.

Conduct research on your committee's prioritized legislation. Is there a similar bill at http://www.senate.gov? (Click to Active Legislation.)

Create a folder with pertinent news articles and Web sites.

Task Number 4: After conducting research, mark up bill and submit for review.

Include additional detail to this bill (e.g., funding).

Is grammar and spelling accurate?

Task Number 5: Begin to prepare for a hearing.

Think of two informed people who could testify in support of certain aspects of this bill and two informed people who could testify against particular aspects of this legislation.

Resource I—Classroom Legislation:
S 125, "Clean Air"

Purpose

To cut down on air pollution, soot, and smog by placing filters on the smoke stacks of all industrial factories and making all city buses and garbage trucks electric.

Provisions

1. All factories must have filters on their smokestacks.

2. Any coal company that does not have enough money to pay for a filter will be eligible for government assistance.

3. If the filter is not installed within a year, the company will be fined $20,000 for the first offense. Upon the second offense, the plant will lose its license and be shut down.

4. This bill will establish a group of inspectors who will go to the plants once every two months to check to see if the law is being followed.

5. If a company is fined (see Provision 3), that money will be used to pay the inspectors (see Provision 4).

6. Fifty percent of all city buses and garbage trucks must be electric within five years.

7. City governments must apply for state assistance to convert their buses to electric power.

8. If a state does not have funding for city governments (see Provisions 6 and 7), it may apply to the federal government for emergency funding.

—Approved by the Committee on
Environmental Affairs

Resource J—Classroom Legislation: S 121, "Reducing Crime"

Purpose

To reduce crime across the United States.

Provisions

1. Reduce the federal health care budget by $5 billion.

2. Transfer $5 billion (see Provision 1) to cities with high crime rates.

3. Give eligible cities money to hire more police officers, develop better training programs, and increase the number of youth centers in urban areas.

4. Have eligible cities raise the salaries of those police officers working in high-crime areas.

—Approved by the Security and
Immigration Committee

Resource K—Testimony: Dr. Van Schick

Hearing: S 121, "Reducing Crime"

Security and Immigration Committee

Dr. Van Schick's Prepared Statement

Hello, my name is Dr. Van Schick. I am a heart surgeon. I have dealt with many old people who do not have enough money to pay for major operations. Health care is one of the most important concerns in people's lives—especially as they get older.

I am here today to state that while I do think that S 121, "Reducing Crime," contains a good idea—we need more police officers on the streets—I do not believe it makes sense to take the money for this program from the health care budget.

If your committee could find another source to obtain this funding, I think it would be a perfect bill.

Resource L—Testimony: Mr. Will Cart

Hearing: S 125, "Clean Air"

Environmental Affairs Committee

Mr. Will Cart's Prepared Statement

My name is Will Cart and I am a 49-year-old man from Fairmont in Marion County, West Virginia. I was a foreman at the Tygart River Mine. We were a very successful mine. We had 20 or more years of coal; I thought I had a secure job. In 1992 I bought a new house and a new car. Now the house has two mortgages, and I sold the car.

Why did all this happen? The 1990 Clean Air Act. One of the provisions said those coal mines producing sulfur dioxide had to get scrubbers in their smoke stacks to reduce the pollution. These scrubbers cost $100 million or more.

Last December we were shut down by the Peabody Holding Company, the largest coal company in the country, for failure to meet the regulations set by the 1990 bill. We couldn't afford a scrubber, so all of us lost our jobs.

When the mine went under, so did the economy of the county. When the 368 miners lost their jobs, 27 retail stores closed, and 400 retail jobs were lost. There is no more demand for supplies.

I have two children living at home and two in college. We could barely send them to school when I was working, but now they will have to drop out.

I want to make it clear. The bill S 125, "Clean Air," is very similar to the disastrous legislation passed in 1990. I am not saying that I am against clean air. I'm completely for it. I just feel that closing every mine down is not the way to achieve it. Coal mines contribute a great amount to the nation's economy and energy. We cannot live without them. Current conditions in our region are the worst they have been since the Great Depression. Isn't there a better way to legislate clean air?

Resource M—Activity: Constructing an Amendment

I, Senator _____, from the state of _____, propose an amendment

to the "_____."
(name of bill)

_____
(title of amendment)

Change the **bill title** to: _____

Change the **purpose** to: _____

_____

Provision 1 (delete or edit): _____

_____

Provision 2 (delete or edit): _____

_____

Provision 3 (delete or edit): _____

_____

Resource N—Excerpts From a Debaters' Handbook

Here is a sample of arguments *in favor of* extending suffrage to women:

The Affirmative is in favor of extending the suffrage to women, for

    I. Woman suffrage is logical and just.
        A. It is the next and last step in the full governmental recognition of woman as a personality.
        B. The right to vote is based on the democratic theory that each one shall have a voice in the government that rules over his affairs.
            1. There can be no true democracy where one-half of the adult population is denied this privilege.
        C. There are many women tax-payers who without the suffrage have no representation in the legislation affecting taxation.
    II. Woman suffrage is expedient.
        A. For the state.
    I. Women are well qualified for the suffrage.
        a. The argument that in order to vote one must be able to fight is unsound.
        b. The percentage of illiterate and foreign-born women is less than the percentage of illiterate and foreign-born men.
        c. Statistics show a similar percentage of criminals, drunkards, etc., among women than among men.

Here is a sample of arguments *against* extending suffrage to women:

The Negative is not in favor of extending the suffrage to women, for

    I. Women cannot claim the vote on the ground of justice.
        A. It is not a natural or inherent right.
            1. It is not so recognized by the Constitution and the Supreme Court.
            2. It is granted for the good of the state and not for the individual.
        B. Voting has nothing to do with taxation.
            1. Many vote who are not taxed.
            2. Many are taxed who may not vote.
        C. Suffrage is not a question of justice, but of policy and expediency.
    II. Woman suffrage would not be expedient.
        A. It would not be for the best interests of society.
            1. Women are unfitted to exercise the franchise.
                a. They are physically unable to enforce the laws.
                b. They are not informed on public questions.
                c. They are swayed by sentiment rather than justice.

Go to http://memory.loc.gov for more arguments.

SOURCE: Phelps (1910).

Glossary

blueprint   Used as a way to organize content or situations within the curriculum drama; see also *pivotal document* and *civic action.*

breaking from   A collective rupture of belief in the curriculum drama, as opposed to *stepping in* to the constructed world of the classroom.

caucus   To "meet together," possibly coming from the Algonquian language group, a language spoken by native people from various tribes in the Northeast region of North America.

civic action   An activity conducted by an informed member(s) of society to further democratic practice (e.g., vote, petition, protest). Used as one type of *blueprint* to frame situations within curriculum drama (e.g., hearing, debate); see also *pivotal document.*

cloture   A procedural strategy used in the senate to limit debate and prevent the possibility of a *filibuster.* For debate to be limited, three-fifths of the senate must vote in favor of it.

curriculum drama   A constructivist approach that builds an "insider's experience" <u>within</u> a defined area of study. Without scripts or predetermined endpoints, the teacher and students construct positions and situations within the constructed world of the classroom; see also *setting the stage* and *multiple entry points.*

double role   When an individual constructs two distinct roles within the curriculum drama (e.g., as a senator and as a witness).

elastic clause   Gives Congress authority to make all "necessary and proper" laws for the federal government (U.S. Constitution, Article 1, section 8).

filibuster   A procedural strategy used to extend debate. This occurs when a legislator delivers an extended speech that prevents a bill from moving forward. To prevent this from happening, the senate might decide to use *cloture.*

hearing   A meeting, usually public, to engage with informed parties over a particular issue. In a legislative hearing, committee members explore a range of testimony directed toward a defined issue or concern. A hearing can serve to inform the committee on legislative details that need revision; see also *markup.*

hopper   A box where bills are placed for consideration by a legislative body, one of many *tools of the trade* used in the classroom senate.

majority party   The party with the most members, counterpart to the *minority party.*

markup   A process where proposed legislation is revised and rewritten; see *hearing.*

minority party   The party whose members do not hold the majority, counterpart to the *majority party.*

multiple entry points   An approach using various ways to entice students to take ownership and build belief in their constructed world; see also *speaking the language.*

party caucus   An informal meeting by a political party to discuss and explore topics of concern; see also *caucus.*

party leader   An individual who guides the party's legislative initiatives through Congress, also called majority leader (leading the *majority party*), or minority leader (leading the *minority party*).

party platform   A document stating the basic views, aims, and priorities of a political party, constructed within a *party caucus.*

party whip   Assists the *party leader* and works to persuade lawmakers to act or vote a particular way on legislative issues.

pivotal document   A written artifact or visual image that can be used to frame content within the curriculum drama. Used as one type of *blueprint;* see also *civic action.*

points of comparison   An approach used within curriculum drama to draw attention to the classroom experience (e.g., classroom senate) and its counterpart in society (U.S. Senate).

president pro tempore   A temporary leader of the U.S. Senate when the vice president of the United States is absent (U.S. Constitution, Article 1, section 3). By custom, this position is given to the longest-serving member of the majority party.

quorum   The number of participants required to be present so as to conduct official business. The U.S. Constitution (Article 1, section 5) requires a simple majority; see also *quorum call.*

quorum call   A procedural strategy used to ensure that a sufficient number of participants are present to conduct official business; see also *quorum.*

setting the stage   An ongoing preparatory process used to lay the groundwork for student ownership, engagement, and leadership.

speaking the language   The practice of deliberately using specialized terms, phrases, and honorific titles in the constructed world of curriculum drama. This language comes from a defined community of practice (e.g., U.S. Senate) that connects to an area of study within the curriculum (e.g., legislative branch of government). This is one of *multiple entry points in curriculum drama.*

stepping in   A collective building of belief in the constructed world of the classroom, as opposed to *breaking from* the curriculum drama.

tools of the trade   Specialized objects used in the constructed world of the classroom. These tools originate from a defined community of practice (e.g., U.S. Senate) that connects to an area of study within the curriculum (e.g., legislative branch of government). This is one of many approaches used in curriculum drama for *setting the stage.*

References

Barone, M., & Cohen, R. (2003). *The almanac of American politics.* Washington, DC: National Journal Group.

Barone, M., & Cohen, R. (2007). *The almanac of American politics 2008.* Washington, DC: National Journal Group.

Bigelow, B. (1998). The people vs. Columbus et al. In B. Bigelow & B. Peterson (Eds.), *Rethinking Columbus* (2nd ed., pp. 87–104). Milwaukee, WI: Rethinking Schools.

Björkman, F. M., & Porritt, A. G. (1917). *"The blue book": Woman suffrage: History arguments and results.* New York: National Woman Suffrage.

Brooks, J., & Brooks, M. (1993). *The case for constructivist classrooms.* Alexandria, VA: Association for Supervision and Curriculum Development.

Byrd, R. (1995). President pro tempore of the senate. In D. Bacon, R. Davidson, & M. Keller (Eds.), *The encyclopedia of the Congress* (Vol. 3, pp. 1604–1610). New York: Simon & Schuster.

Dahl, R. (2003). *How democratic is the American Constitution?* New Haven, CT: Yale University Press.

Dewey, J. (1934). *Art as experience.* New York: Minton, Balch.

Franklin, C. (2001). *Being there: Active imaginations and inquiring minds in a middle school classroom.* Unpublished dissertation. Teachers College, Columbia University.

Franklin, C. (2003, March). Curriculum drama: Using imagination and inquiry in a middle school social studies classroom. *Occasional Paper Series* #10. New York: Bank Street College of Education.

Franklin, C. (2005). "Being there: Middle school students as coconstructors of a classroom senate." In C. Fosnot (Ed.), *Constructivism: Theory, perspective, and practice.* New York: Teachers College Press.

Freire, P. (1973). *Education for critical consciousness.* New York: Continuum.

Freire, P. (1996). *Letters to Cristina: Reflections on my life and work.* New York: Routledge.

Fulton, J. D. (1869). *The true woman: A series of discourses: to which is added woman vs. ballot.* Boston: Lee and Shepard.

Greene, M. (1995). *Releasing the imagination.* San Francisco: Jossey-Bass.

Greene, M. (2001). *Variations on a blue guitar.* New York: Teachers College Press.

Greene, M. (2005). A constructivist perspective on teaching and learning in the arts. In C. Fosnot (Ed.), *Constructivism: Theory, perspective, and practice* (pp. 110–131). New York: Teachers College Press.

Greeno, J. G. (1991). Number sense as situated knowing in a conceptual domain. *Journal for Research in Mathematics Education, 22*(3), 170–218.

Heathcote, D. (1984). The authentic teacher and the future. In L. Johnson & C. O'Neill (Eds.), *Dorothy Heathcote: Collected writings on education and drama* (pp. 170–199). Evanston, IL: Northwestern University Press.

Heathcote, D., & Herbert, P. (1985). A drama of learning: Mantle of the expert. *Theory into Practice, 24*(3), 173–180.

International Reading Association and the National Council of Teachers of English. (1996). *Standards for the English language arts.* Urbana IL: Authors.

Juvonen, J., Le, V., Kaganoff, T., Augustine, C., & Constant, L. (2004). *Focus on the wonder years: Challenges facing the American middle school.* Arlington, VA: Rand Corporation.

Kilborn, P. T. (1996, February 15). East's coal towns wither in the name of clean air. *The New York Times* [Electronic version]. Retrieved June 13, 2008, from http://query.nytimes.com/gst/fullpage.html?res=9C03E7D91239F936 A25751C0A960958260

Kuhn, D. (1986). Education for thinking. *Teachers College Record, 87*(4), 495–512.

Lambert, L. (1995). Leading the conversations. In L. Lambert, D. Walker, D. Zimmerman, J. Cooper, M. Lambert, M. Gardner, et al. (Eds.), *The constructivist leader* (pp. 82–103). New York: Teachers College Press.

Lave, J., & Wenger, E. (1991*). Situated learning: Legitimate peripheral participation.* Cambridge, UK: Cambridge University Press.

Madison, G. (1988). *The hermeneutics of postmodernity: Figures and themes.* Bloomington: Indiana University Press.

National Council for the Social Studies. (1994). *Curriculum standards for social studies: Expectations for excellence.* Washington, DC: Author.

Neill, M. (2003, September). Low expectations and less learning: The problem with No Child Left Behind. *Social Education, 67*(4), 281–284.

No Child Left Behind Act, 20 USC §§ 6301 *et seq.* (2005).

O'Neill, C. (1995). *Drama worlds. A framework for process drama.* Portsmouth, NH: Heinemann.

Oxford American dictionary. (1980). New York: Oxford University Press.

Phelps, E. M. (Compiler). (1910). *Selected articles on woman suffrage, comp. by Edith M. Phelps.* Minneapolis, MN: H. W. Wilson.

Schifter, D., & Fosnot, C. (1993). *Reconstructing mathematics education: Stories of teachers meeting the challenge of reform.* New York: Teachers College Press.

Stanton, E. C. (1915). *Solitude of self: Address delivered by Mrs. Stanton before the Committee of the Judiciary of the United States Congress, Monday, January 18, 1892.* Washington, DC: Government Printing Office.

United States Senate. (n.d.). *Oath of office.* Retrieved May 27, 2008, from http://www.senate.gov/artandhistory/history/common/briefing/ Oath_Office.htm

VanFossen, P. (2005). "Reading and math take so much of the time . . . ": An overview of social studies instruction in elementary classrooms in Indiana. *Theory and Research in Social Education. 33*(3), 376–403.

von Zastrow, C., & Janc, H. (2004, March). *Academic atrophy: The condition of the liberal arts in America's public schools.* Washington, DC: Council for Basic Education.

Wagner, B. (1976). *Dorothy Heathcote: Drama as a learning medium.* Washington, DC: National Education Association.

Ward, W. (1957). *Playmaking with children from kindergarten through junior high school.* New York: Appleton-Century-Crofts.

Wenger, E. (1998). *Communities of practice: Learning, meaning, and identity.* Cambridge, UK: Cambridge University Press.

Wolf, S. (1995). Language in and around the dramatic curriculum. *Journal of Curriculum Studies, 27,* 118–137.

Zinn, H. (2003). *A people's history of the United States: 1492–present.* New York: Harper Collins.

Zinn, H., & Arnov, A. (2004). *Voices of a people's history of the United States.* New York: Seven Stories Press.

Electronic References Cited in This Text

American Memory—The Library of Congress

http://memory.loc.gov

Congressional Biographical Directory

http://bioguide.congress.gov

Democratic National Committee

http://www.democrats.org

Doctors Without Borders

http://www.doctorswithoutborders.org

Habitat for Humanity International

http://www.habitat.org

Humane Society

http://www.hsus.org

National Association for the Advancement of Colored People

http://www.naacp.org

National Council of Teachers of English

http://www.ncte.org

National Council for the Social Studies

  http://www.socialstudies.org

National Journal—The Almanac of American Politics

  http://www.nationaljournal.com/almanac

Republican National Committee

  http://www.gop.com

U.S. Senate Democrats

  http://www.democrats.senate.gov

U.S. Senate Republicans

  http://www.republican.senate.gov

U.S. Senate

  http://www.senate.gov

Women's International League for Peace and Freedom

  http://www.wilpf.org

50 states

  http://www.50states.com

Index